WIN

THE BIG MATCH

Julian Pottage

BATSFORD

2-05 16.95

First published 2004

© Julian Pottage 2004

The right of Julian Pottage to be identified as Author of this work has been asserted by him in accordance with the Copyright, Designs and Patents Act 1988.

ISBN 0 7134 8922 7

A CIP catalogue record for this book is available from the British Library.

Typeset in the U.K. by Ruth Edmondson
Printed in the U.K. by Creative Print & Design, Ebbw Vale, Wales

for the publishers

B T Batsford, The Chrysalis Building, Bramley Road, London W10 6SP

An imprint of **Chrysalis** Books Group

Distributed in the United States and Canada by Sterling Publishing Co., 387 Park Avenue South, New York, NY 10016, USA

Editor: Elena Jeronimidis

CONTENTS

ACKNOWLEDGMENTS

Firstly, I would like to thank those involved in the book's production, especially Ruth Edmondson, Tony Gordon and Elena Jeronimidis.

Next, I would like to thank everybody who checked and made helpful suggestions about my initial manuscript, principally Graham Allan and Maureen Dennison.

The material itself I do not need to credit, though for the benefit of the readers who are interested, I shall explain its source anyway. The majority of the deals are my own compositions, usually built up from a single point or strategy in the play. The remainder mainly consists of reworked examples from *Bridge Plus, Bridge Magazine* and the *Daily Bridge Calendar* (there is also one from Richard Pavlicek's web site). I hasten to add that I changed the deals as originally published not to avoid the need to seek permission for their use (which I am confident I would have been able to obtain) but rather to illustrate better my chosen purpose – such as making the key point clearer or conforming the bidding to contemporary standards.

Finally, I would like to rectify an omission that dates back twenty-one years. None of my earliest books included a credits page, with the result that many people are unaware of who it was who inspired me to start collecting material for inclusion in a book, and who introduced me to someone willing to publish it, and how grateful I am to each of them. The former is Richard Plackett, my partner in Cambridge's win in the 1983 Varsity match and in England's victory in the 1984 Junior Camrose. The latter is Patrick Jourdain, who for many years was Secretary to the International Bridge Press Association (now President) and responsible for the monthly IBPA newsletter. Both Richard and Patrick have won the Gold Cup and it therefore seems particularly fitting to dedicate this book to them. If I may, perhaps I can also include in the dedication all those whose best result in the competition is runner-up!

INTRODUCTION

Well done! You have made it to the final of the Gold Cup, the most prestigious bridge event in Great Britain. To lift the trophy you face one last hurdle – to win a tough match against another team with the same aspiration. To do so you will need to come through a number of bidding decisions and find the winning line of play or defensive strategy about half the time. A head-to-head match is a special form of competition but do not worry if this is unfamiliar to you as I am about to explain it. If you are used to playing teams, you may wish to skip to the top of page 7.

As in duplicate pairs, your score is not absolute; whether it is good or bad depends on what happens elsewhere – in this case the other table. Again, as in duplicate pairs, you play cards in front of you, rather than the middle of the table, and at the end of the play put them in a board or wallet designed for the purpose. The markings on the board give the dealer and the vulnerability and you cannot carry forward a part score from one deal to another. There are bonuses for part scores, games and slams to be added to the trick score (for details see page 153) but otherwise the score is like playing a series of single deal rubbers.

At any one time, each team has one pair playing North-South and another playing East-West; then, after they have played a specified number of deals, they will meet up and compare scores. The vast majority of team events use a scoring method known as International Match Points, IMPs for short. So, having added the pairs of scores on a board together, you convert the aggregate difference into IMPs (see page 157 for the conversion table and 158 for some sample scores).

The fact that the size of the swing matters puts a premium on making your contract or defeating the opponents', especially if it is a game or slam. So, in the play of the cards, you normally adopt the same sort of tactics as you would playing rubber bridge. Although in theory a large number of 1 IMP swings from making an overtrick missed in the other room can add up, it rarely pays to strive for them. For one thing, few matches are won or lost by a handful of IMPs. For another, especially in a long match (this one consists of 64 boards – eight or nine hour's play) you will need to save your energy for the more difficult boards.

You will be relieved to hear that you do not just sit down against one pair and play 64 boards without a break. Instead, the match divides into sets (or stanzas), normally of eight boards. After each set you may change room or opponents. Also, if you are playing in a team of more than four – a good idea in a lengthy match – you may change who is sitting out.

Usually (and it will be so here), the match consists of an even number of sets and the sides take turns to have seating rights. When you have seating rights, you wait for the opponents to announce where they intend to sit and determine your line-up accordingly. If they have seating rights, the converse applies – you announce your line-up and then they choose theirs. The team captains decide how to exercise seating rights and which members of their team will sit out for each set. A good captain will only do this having ascertained which members of the team are ready and raring to go (your ideal status), which need some rest, and if anyone has a preference about whom and where to play.

Playing against people you do not know, you might change opponents (or room) if you have lost IMPs in a particular set or try to keep as much as possible the same if you have been doing well. However, when playing against people you know, or have done some homework about, different factors might affect your choices. For example, one pair in your team might feel more comfortable than the others about playing against a strong club system. Or maybe you like to play against people of a similar age and gender or philosophy as yourselves. Alternatively, you may know from past experience which opponents inspire you to play well and which always seem to find a way of fixing you.

In an important match like a Gold Cup final, one room will be the 'open' and the other the 'closed'. Spectators may watch in the open room but only the players and match officials may enter the closed room. Some people find that having an audience sharpens their game while others find the greater noise and hubbub in the open room a distraction.

In a prestigious match like this, the match officials typically consist of three people, two recording what happens at each table and one with a largely passive role as Director. The latter assumes responsibility for ensuring that the speed of play meets the conditions specified for the competition (often quite a generous 70 minutes for eight boards) and for making sure that both tables have the right boards and that the players are sitting in their correct positions. In theory, the Director also handles any irregularities but, in practice, they rarely arise.

Contrary to what some cynics might suggest, most matches are played in a pleasant atmosphere, highly competitive but respectful and, away from the table, players from opposing teams can be the best of friends. Even at the table, it would be quite common for a player ordering a round of drinks to include the opposing pair in the order. For this reason I intend to refer to players on both sides by first names only. (At times I may refer to members of the opposing team as 'he' or 'she'.)

The Cast

The opposing team are slightly surprise finalists and comprises three pairs: Edgar and Steve, Lucy and Suzanne, and Wayne and Sally.

Edgar, their captain, is a partner in a city legal firm. He is the perfect gentleman and always smartly dressed. Nobody knows his age exactly but you estimate it at around 60. Edgar likes playing East or North.

Steve, Edgar's partner, works as a doctor, a general practitioner, and is considerably younger than Edgar – in his late 30s or perhaps 40. He has four children back home and dresses in more casual attire. Edgar and Steve play less often than their other pairs, but when they do it is mainly rubber bridge, for high stakes I might add. This means that their card play is sound and that their bidding sequences tend to be short and simple and largely free of gadgets.

Lucy has recently retired as headteacher of a secondary school. She is calm and confident and an experienced player. If you could see Lucy's outfit, you might say that she dresses more for comfort than for fashion!

Suzanne now has slightly more time than she used to for devoting to bridge. During the 1980s, she established a chain of health food shops across the North of England. She tries to look a little younger than she actually is (perhaps the healthy eating has something to do with it!) and has won several major bridge events with Lucy. Suzanne, who likes playing South or East, is the one more prone to flights of fancy but you know from her success away from the table that she must judge most situations well. Lucy and Suzanne are their only pair using a weak no-trump, and the only ones who might, in theory, open a four-card major.

Wayne stands out from the others in their team from the way he looks. Indoors and out, it seems he always wears his cap, so either he wishes to cover up premature balding or he is the world's biggest Red Sox fan. Designer label or not, his jeans and tee-shirt give little clue to his job as an investment manager for the First National Bank of Boston.

Like Wayne, Sally is also in her late 20s or perhaps just turned thirty. You are told that she works as a computer programmer but it is hard to avoid thinking that she missed her calling as a model or an actress. She has a perfect figure, fair hair gently lapping on her shoulders, big blue eyes and a warm smile. Were it not for the enormous diamond ring that Wayne obviously gave her, an unattached male might find it difficult to concentrate on the bridge with her as an opponent!

Wayne and Sally play a natural bidding system, with five-card majors and a strong no-trump (like their all-male pair) but with many of the latest conventions (like the women) and slightly more of an American influence, particularly on the leads (sometimes top of nothing from small cards and king from ace-king).

Your team also comprises three pairs: Chris, the captain, and Alex, Phil and Sam, and you and Pat. You can decide which, if any, of your team are male and which, if any, are female. You all play similar systems and you will be relieved to hear that your team does not feel out of its depth at this level. You can hope for a fair share of good results from the other table and a sympathetic ear for the odd disaster at yours!

Playing on a team of six, you might anticipate the occasional break – but do not count on it! Everyone else on your team regards you and Pat as the strongest pair. Moreover, Chris, the captain, thinks that you both have the stamina of Ethiopian marathon runners.

Normally you might expect to play some time in the open room and some time in the closed. Again, special circumstances apply. Pat, though mentally as sharp as ever, now finds it difficult to get up and down stairs – a task that playing in the closed room would involve. This means that when you play (and you are not expecting to sit out) you will do so as South in the open room. Sportingly, Edgar has agreed that in spite of this he will allow your team to choose opponents on alternate sets as usual.

You and Pat have been playing together for a while and get on well. You play a variable no-trump, with a range of 12-14 non-vulnerable and 15-17 when vulnerable, and five-card majors. You use all the conventions that have become standard in the tournament world: to name but two, splinters and Roman Key Card Blackwood. Anything out of the ordinary that you might need to know I shall clarify as we go along.

For the first round, your team has choice of opponents, although the matter largely rests out of your hands. Pat, despite being no spring chicken, can still find it intimidating to play against two strong, mature, women players. Also, at this early stage, neither of you wishes to take on a pair who seem to produce better results than their ability as individuals suggest they should. So, as Edgar and Steve are playing in the first round, you will do battle against them.

As you take up your seats and exchange convention cards (showing your bidding and carding methods) and pleasantries, you hope nothing too dramatic will happen on the first board . . .

> **South (You)**
> ♠ K 6 5
> ♡ —
> ◇ 10 6 5
> ♣ Q 10 8 6 5 4 3

Pat, North, opens 1◇ and East, passes. Playing inverted raises (where 2◇ is strong), a raise is out. A 1♠ response may cause big problems, and a pass makes it too easy for West to bid, so you try 1NT (you might get a chance to bid clubs later to show that you have a long clubs in a hand too weak for a two-level response). This succeeds in silencing the opponents, and Pat raises to 3NT. You could leave this, but two dangers may arise. For one, a heart lead could prove deadly. For another, you may have too few entries to enjoy the clubs. 4♣ here should show more than 5♣ (inviting a cue-bid), so this is the auction:

West	North	East	South
Steve	*Pat*	*Edgar*	*You*
	1◇	Pass	1NT
Pass	3NT	Pass	5♣
All Pass			

Steve, West, scribbles something indecipherable on his score-card and leads the ♠7. When dummy appears, you see that you did the right thing in removing 3NT. How you do plan the play?

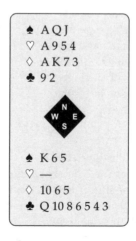

> ♠ A Q J
> ♡ A 9 5 4
> ◇ A K 7 3
> ♣ 9 2
>
> **N W E S**
>
> ♠ K 6 5
> ♡ —
> ◇ 10 6 5
> ♣ Q 10 8 6 5 4 3

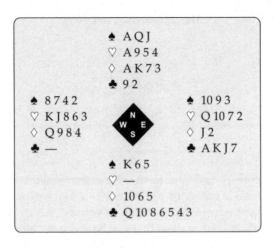

♠ A Q J
♡ A 9 5 4
♢ A K 7 3
♣ 9 2

♠ 8 7 4 2
♡ K J 8 6 3
♢ Q 9 8 4
♣ —

♠ 10 9 3
♡ Q 10 7 2
♢ J 2
♣ A K J 7

♠ K 6 5
♡ —
♢ 10 6 5
♣ Q 10 8 6 5 4 3

The ♡A will take care of your third-round diamond loser, so you focus on restricting your trump losers to two. This will prove easy enough if they split 2-2 or East has A-K-J. You can also do it if West has a bare jack by leading to the queen. A bare ace or king with him is, however, more likely, so you do better to finesse if East follows with the seven. You also stand a chance if East has four trumps. Then, of course, you will need a trump coup – luckily, dummy has quite a few entries.

To bring off a trump coup you will need to ruff three times in hand, reducing your trump length to East's. You will also need to lead trumps twice from dummy. More difficult to spot is that it may prove critical whether you lead the ♣9 on the first round or the second.

Suppose you win the spade in dummy and lead the ♣9. East does best to go in with ace and exit safely with a spade. You can then use dummy's remaining entries to ruff three hearts in hand and get back there for trick eleven. In the position shown Edgar will duck the club and you will be stuck in the wrong hand, forced to concede the last two tricks.

♠ —
♡ —
♢ 7 3
♣ 2

♠ 8
♡ —
♢ Q 9
♣ —

♠ —
♡ —
♢ —
♣ K J 7

♠ —
♡ —
♢ —
♣ Q 10 8

The solution is to lead the low club first. Then, if necessary, you will be able to hold the lead in dummy for trick twelve. It does not matter if East ducks the first trump, as he will then win the eleventh trick and be the one endplayed. 'Too good for me,' Edgar will say if you got this one right.

Win the Big Match

BOARD 2   Dealer: East. N/S Vulnerable.

South (You)
♠ K J 7 6 5 3
♡ Q
◊ A K Q 6
♣ K 5

You open 1♠ in second seat and Pat responds 1NT. What do you rebid? 2◊ may end the bidding with game cold. The same applies to 3♠; indeed this could turn out worse, as 3♠ might fail with 3NT or 5◊ makeable. A four-loser hand with 18 points in high cards entitles you to use a game-forcing jump to 3◊ and Pat gives preference to 3♠. Your shape suggests a 6-2 fit will play better than 3NT, so you raise to 4♠.

West	North	East	South
Steve	*Pat*	*Edgar*	*You*
		Pass	1♠
Pass	1NT	Pass	3◊
Pass	3♠	Pass	4♠
All Pass			

West leads the ♡10, and you see you have reached the right spot.

East wins the first heart with the king and, after adjusting his smart striped tie, returns the ace, which you ruff. How should you continue?

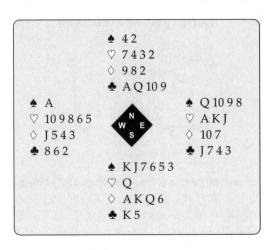

♠ 4 2
♡ 7 4 3 2
◇ 9 8 2
♣ A Q 10 9

♠ A
♡ 10 9 8 6 5
◇ J 5 4 3
♣ 8 6 2

♠ Q 10 9 8
♡ A K J
◇ 10 7
♣ J 7 4 3

♠ K J 7 6 5 3
♡ Q
◇ A K Q 6
♣ K 5

Diamonds may break 3-3, turning your small diamond into a winner. If not, you might discard it on a club. You cannot readily test diamonds, but you know you would rather rely on clubs 4-3 (if you have to run the clubs before drawing trumps) than diamonds 3-3, so that settles one issue. You now turn your mind to the risk of losing three trump tricks.

You need not worry about a heart overruff, as with six hearts headed by the ace-king-jack Edgar surely would have bid either as dealer or over the 1NT response. So, what are the main dangers to consider?

If West, Steve, has ace, queen and another spade then you cannot do anything about it. Nor can you cater for a singleton ace on your right. If you lead twice towards the king-jack, you would avoid having to guess whether East has Q-x-x or A-x-x. Sadly, leading from dummy twice means overtaking the ♣K with the ace, so you would need to finesse the ♣10 to make three club tricks. Thankfully, you can avoid that.

Edgar, who passed as dealer, can hardly have the ♠A in addition to ♡A-K-J. This tells you (assuming the contract has a chance) that you only need one entry to dummy, and you should use this for leading to the jack rather than the king. So, should you do this on the first round of the suit, or is it better to start by leading low from hand?

Ducking the first round of spades offers two advantages. For one, if you play three rounds of clubs and then a spade to the jack and ace, a deadly trump promotion will result if West has three spades and four clubs; in that scenario, East can ruff the fourth round of clubs with the ♠Q. For another, West may have a bare ♠A, as is actually the case.

BOARD 3   Dealer: South. E/W Vulnerable.

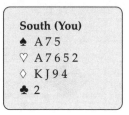

South (You)
♠ A 7 5
♡ A 7 6 5 2
◇ K J 9 4
♣ 2

You open 1♡ and Pat responds 3♠. Edgar politely inquires what this means and you say that you play this as splinter: a raise to game with four-card (or better) trump support and a singleton or void spade. Edgar overcalls 4♠, and it is tempting to double; however, you should beware of acting too quickly. Both sides may have a 10-card fit, in which case you do not want to defend at the four level. Luckily, you do not have to decide. A forcing pass allows Pat to express an opinion.

With 0-5 or 1-4 in the majors, Pat will bid 5♡ or double respectively. With 0-4 or 1-5 in the majors partner will have to assess the offensive and defensive potential of the rest of the hand to decide what to do. In practice, Pat doubles to end the auction.

West	North	East	South
Steve	*Pat*	*Edgar*	*You*
			1♡
Pass	3♠	4♠	Pass
Pass	Double	All Pass	

You lead the ♣2, dummy plays low, and partner's ten fetches the ace.

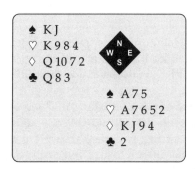

♠ K J
♡ K 9 8 4
◇ Q 10 7 2
♣ Q 8 3

♠ A 7 5
♡ A 7 6 5 2
◇ K J 9 4
♣ 2

At trick two, declarer leads a small trump. What are your plans?

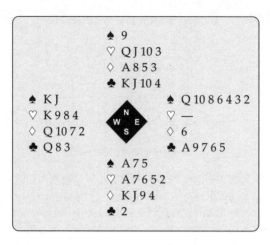

```
              ♠ 9
              ♡ Q J 10 3
              ◇ A 8 5 3
              ♣ K J 10 4
♠ K J                        ♠ Q 10 8 6 4 3 2
♡ K 9 8 4        N           ♡ —
◇ Q 10 7 2    W     E        ◇ 6
♣ Q 8 3          S           ♣ A 9 7 6 5
              ♠ A 7 5
              ♡ A 7 6 5 2
              ◇ K J 9 4
              ♣ 2
```

You can read the club position from the play to trick one. North needs the
♣K to have enough to raise to game and Edgar would have taken the ten
with the jack if he could. For the first of these reasons, Pat must also have
the ◇A. Edgar, who hardly possesses a reputation as an adventurous
bidder, must have a very shapely hand to bid 4♠ on 6 points vulnerable
against not and knowing trumps might break badly.

If he is 8-0-0-5, you have done the wrong thing in defending, since you
can only score two clubs and a trump. Of course, such a shape occurs
rarely. Conversely, if Edgar is 7-0-2-4, you are going to pick up 800: three
tricks in the black suits, two top diamonds and a club ruff will give you
six tricks. However, in view of the weakness of his spades and the
vulnerability, you expect him to have more shape than that.

Most likely Edgar has 12 black cards rather than 11 or 13, giving him
either a 7-0-1-5 or 8-0-1-4 shape. In both cases, your play to the first
round of trumps may prove crucial. Do you see why?

Declarer knows the club position as well as you do. If you allow him to
reach dummy, he will lead the ♡K and discard his singleton diamond.
Then bang goes your link to Pat and your club ruff with it!

Taking the infinitesimal risk of crashing the bare ♠Q, you hop up with
the ♠A, put Pat in with the ◇A and collect your club ruff. Happily, it
matters not whether partner underleads the ♣K to give you a ruff on the
second round or cashes the ♣K to give you a ruff on the third. Either way
you will exit safely with your remaining trump and wait for Edgar to
lose gracefully whatever club tricks he has to.

BOARD 4   Dealer: West. Game All.

```
┌─────────────────────────┐
│  South (You)            │
│  ♠ J 10 8 5 3 2         │
│  ♡ 10                   │
│  ◊ 3                    │
│  ♣ K 7 6 5 2           │
└─────────────────────────┘
```

Steve, West, opens 3♡, and Pat makes a take-out double. Edgar, East, fumbles slightly in his bidding box, presumably looking for a card he does not use very often. Out comes a blue card: redouble.

With such terrific distribution, the lack of high cards should not deter you from your intended bid of 4♠. Using the losing trick count, you find only 7 losers – the same as for a typical opening bid!

The next two players pass and, with an air of reluctance, East does the same. Presumably, he has decided that the redouble showed his hand.

West	North	East	South
Steve	*Pat*	*Edgar*	*You*
3♡	Dbl	Redbl	4♠
All Pass			

West leads the ♡Q and dummy looks okay. How you do plan the play?

```
♠ Q 9 7 4
♡ A K 5
◊ A 9 7 6 5
♣ Q

♠ J 10 8 5 3 2
♡ 10
◊ 3
♣ K 7 6 5 2
```

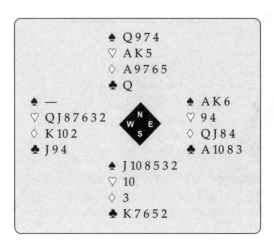

You count four trump tricks, three top winners in the red suits and, after driving out the ace, one club winner. This means that taking two ruffs in dummy will see you home. Unfortunately, if you play a club and trumps split 3-0, it seems likely that Edgar will be able to draw three rounds of trumps, leaving you a winner short. You will also lack sufficient entries to set up either minor and be unable to exert any real pressure even if the same defender (East no doubt) has four cards in each minor.

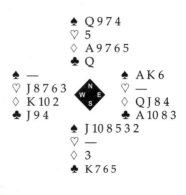

The answer is to start with ace, king and a third round of hearts. If East has a 3-2-4-4 shape, he will be in big trouble. If he weakens his holding in one of the minors then you will be able to set up the suit by ruffing. If, instead, he ruffs, you can overruff and drive out the ♣A knowing he cannot draw dummy's trumps. No ambiguity arises, as the squeeze that you need with trumps 3-0 only works if East has length in both minors.

True, if Edgar has 3-2 in the majors and unequal minors, he will have a safe discard on the third heart, but then you are always going down.

Oddly enough, playing two top hearts also works if, unexpectedly, East holds a 3-1-5-4 shape. He has to ruff, or a third round will squeeze him as above, but you will overruff; this then gives you the capability to ruff two clubs in dummy, setting up a long card as you do so.

BOARD 5   Dealer: North. N/S Vulnerable.

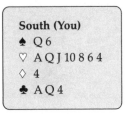

South (You)
♠ Q 6
♡ A Q J 10 8 6 4
◊ 4
♣ A Q 4

You open 1♡, Steve doubles and Pat jumps to 3♡, showing a hand worth a normal raise to 2♡ and guaranteeing four trumps. East on your right passes and your advance to 4♡ buys the contract.

West	North	East	South
Steve	*Pat*	*Edgar*	*You*
	Pass	Pass	1♡
Dbl	3♡	Pass	4♡
All Pass			

Steve scrawls something illegible on his score-card again (you have worked out this must be the contract) and, when he leads the ♠A, dummy's doubleton spade comes as a bit of a surprise. Rarely do you buy the contract below four of their suit when total trumps equal 20 (you have an 11-card heart fit and they have nine spades) and you can hope for even breaks, trumps 1-1 for example.

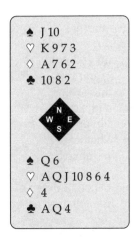

♠ J 10
♡ K 9 7 3
◊ A 7 6 2
♣ 10 8 2

♠ Q 6
♡ A Q J 10 8 6 4
◊ 4
♣ A Q 4

Edgar plays low but Steve cashes a second top spade and, seeing the nine from his partner, shifts to the ◊Q. How do you play from here?

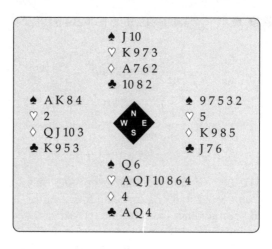

♠ J 10
♡ K 9 7 3
♢ A 7 6 2
♣ 10 8 2

♠ A K 8 4   ♠ 9 7 5 3 2
♡ 2   ♡ 5
♢ Q J 10 3   ♢ K 9 8 5
♣ K 9 5 3   ♣ J 7 6

♠ Q 6
♡ A Q J 10 8 6 4
♢ 4
♣ A Q 4

Presumably, the missing spades are 4-5, or Steve might have chosen a 1♠ overcall. This tells you the club finesse stands little chance. With five spades and king of both minors, surely Edgar would have bid 3♠ (you suspect that Chris, your team-mate, might bid it with just one king).

Clearly, a throw-in offers the best prospect of enabling you to avoid the loss of two club tricks, so you put up dummy's ace and ruff a diamond high to begin the elimination. You continue with a middle trump to the king, pleased to see all follow, and ruff another diamond high.

This is the position after you have gone back to dummy. You had hoped Edgar would have only three diamonds, in which case you could have thrown a club on the fourth round and claimed. As the cards lie, you must ruff and go back to dummy with a trump. It would be a mistake now to finesse the ♣Q. If this loses to the king and a club comes back (as will surely happen), you will have a 50-50 guess whether to play the eight or the ten from dummy.

♠ —
♡ 7 3
♢ 7
♣ 10 8 2

♠ 8   ♠ 7 5
♡ —   ♡ —
♢ J   ♢ K
♣ K 9 5 3   ♣ J 7 6

♠ —
♡ 10 6 4
♢ —
♣ A Q 4

To avoid this problem, lead the eight or ten of clubs, intending to run it. If East produces the card immediately above this, at least you spare yourself a guess. If not, the contract becomes 100%. If Edgar has J-9 and Steve the king then that is just too bad.

BOARD 6   Dealer: East. E/W Vulnerable.

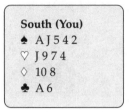

```
South (You)
♠ A J 5 4 2
♡ J 9 7 4
◇ 10 8
♣ A 6
```

Edgar opens 1♣. What do you call? With 5-4 in the majors and 2-2 in the minors, it usually works better to overcall in your five-card suit than to make a take-out double. The danger of missing a 5-3 in your long suit if you do not bid it roughly equates to the one of missing a 4-4 fit in your secondary suit if you do. This makes the risk of an unwelcome response in your short suit the deciding factor. In any event, you would prefer more values than this to double.

Steve jumps to 2NT over 1♠, a bid normally showing a good 10 up to a poor 12 and Edgar raises to 3NT.

West	North	East	South
Steve	*Pat*	*Edgar*	*You*
		1♣	1♠
2NT	Pass	3NT	All Pass

Pat leads the ♠9, and dummy comes down with what about you would guess, a balanced hand fractionally too weak for a strong no-trump.

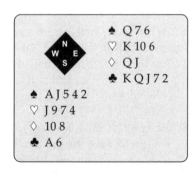

```
          ♠ Q 7 6
          ♡ K 10 6
          ◇ Q J
          ♣ K Q J 7 2
♠ A J 5 4 2
♡ J 9 7 4
◇ 10 8
♣ A 6
```

Declarer, after stroking his chin a couple of times, calls for a low card and you must decide what to do.

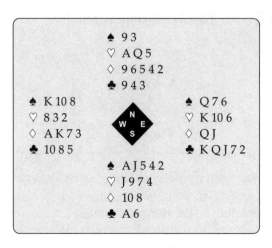

```
              ♠ 9 3
              ♡ A Q 5
              ◇ 9 6 5 4 2
              ♣ 9 4 3
♠ K 10 8                      ♠ Q 7 6
♡ 8 3 2          N            ♡ K 10 6
◇ A K 7 3    W     E          ◇ Q J
♣ 10 8 5         S            ♣ K Q J 7 2
              ♠ A J 5 4 2
              ♡ J 9 7 4
              ◇ 10 8
              ♣ A 6
```

To take the ♠A and return the suit would be defeatist. On the bidding (and lead – as a rule, you lead middle from three low whether or not the suit has been bid), you place declarer with three spades (at least), so this would serve to cut your communications with partner.

Ducking the first spade sounds much better. If Pat gets in first (and still has a spade to lead), it will be possible to drive out your opponent's second stopper. Then, when you get in with the ♣A, the spades will be ready to run. The snag is that declarer may find it more natural to set up dummy's long suit before doing anything else, and this will remove your entry prematurely. You can reasonably predict that if Pat has the ◇K then Steve will want to dislodge the ♣A before taking the diamond finesse, since he knows that you cannot win an early diamond trick.

Could taking the first trick and switching to a red suit work? For a diamond to do any good, you probably need Pat to hold a seven-card suit headed by the ace, but this sounds most unlikely. Surely, a heart shift offers better odds. In this case, you just need to find partner with A-Q-x (or, of course, A-Q-x-x). This does not seem so much to ask.

You may also defeat the contract after leading a heart if partner has ♡Q-x-x and the ◇A. Steve will need to guess which way round the minor-suit aces sit. If he plays on diamonds before clubs, he may well lose two hearts and three aces. Admittedly, if the cards lie that way then you might also succeed by ducking the first spade.

On the actual layout, Pat wins the first heart with the ace and returns the queen, leaving declarer without recourse.

BOARD 7   Dealer: South. Game All.

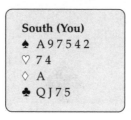

South (You)
♠ A 9 7 5 4 2
♡ 7 4
◇ A
♣ Q J 7 5

You open 1♠, partner raises to 2♠ and Edgar, East, overcalls 3♡. The sixth spade entitles you to compete to the three level, as you can be sure of a nine-card fit. 3♠ does not invite game – double would do that. Steve on your left goes 4♡ and this come back to you. It would breach partnership discipline to call 4♠ now – you have bid your hand already, and for all you know 4♠ doubled might go for 800 with 4♡ due to fail. (In some circles a phantom costing more than the potential value of the opposing contract is known as a 'Granville Sacrifice'.)

West	North	East	South
Steve	*Pat*	*Edgar*	*You*
			1♠
Pass	2♠	3♡	3♠
4♡	All Pass		

The singleton ◇A is an easy lead and, having led it, you see this:

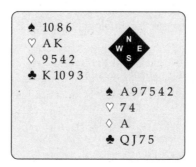

♠ 10 8 6
♡ A K
◇ 9 5 4 2
♣ K 10 9 3

♠ A 9 7 5 4 2
♡ 7 4
◇ A
♣ Q J 7 5

Your ace collects the two, eight and three, and you switch to a middle spade. Partner wins with the queen, the jack falling on your right, and returns the ◇10. Declarer covers with the jack and you ruff. Assuming Pat would not raise 1♠ to 2♠ with ♠K-Q bare, how do you continue?

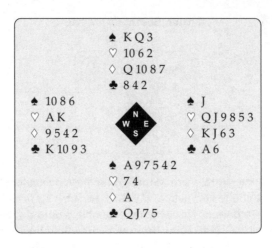

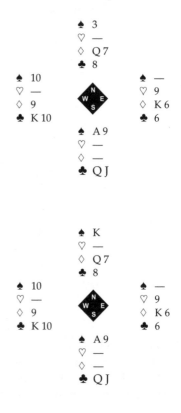

To try a low spade next would be fraught with danger. If the ♠8 draws the king and declarer ruffs, you will take on sole control of spades.

After unblocking the ♡A-K, Edgar returns to hand with a club and finishes the trumps (see right). You can spare a spade and dummy a diamond, but you have no discard when the ◊K appears. The squeeze would also hit you if declarer had a 1-5-4-3 shape with ◊K-Q-J-x. Clearly, a club switch at trick four is out of the question and it might seem you do better to lead the ♠A, but that merely passes the problem across the table.

Left in charge of trying to beat the ♠10, partner would be squeezed in spades and diamonds after declarer runs the trumps and goes to the ♣K. The answer is to exit passively with a trump. This way you will reach an end position like the one shown. On the last trump you can spare a spade and Pat a club. Declarer can only force one of you to unguard spades by cashing a king, but then he lacks an entry for completing the squeeze.

South (You)
♠ K 3
♡ 8 6
♢ A 7
♣ A K J 10 7 6 3

Steve, on your left, opens 4♡, and this comes round to you. Although you might fare better defending, any bid other than 5♣ risks producing a silly result. Most experts play that after an opposing pre-empt you can place partner with roughly a balanced 8-count, which should give 5♣ play. Pat, obviously with a better hand than that, raises you to 6♣.

West	North	East	South
Steve	*Pat*	*Edgar*	*You*
4♡	Pass	Pass	5♣
Pass	6♣	All Pass	

West leads the ♡K and you think you can count eleven tricks on top:

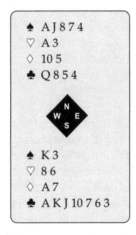

♠ A J 8 7 4
♡ A 3
♢ 10 5
♣ Q 8 5 4

♠ K 3
♡ 8 6
♢ A 7
♣ A K J 10 7 6 3

A recount becomes necessary when Edgar, almost apologetically, ruffs dummy's ♡A at trick one! He returns the ♢J and, thankfully, the second red ace stands up, West following low. Steve does not, however, follow suit when you lay down the ♣A. How do you continue?

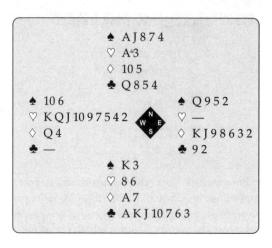

Having lost the ruff, you require four spade tricks to bring the tally up to twelve. Moreover, since you cannot afford to lose the lead, you must attack the suit yourself. Ordinarily with this combination you would cash the king and ace, then ruff the third round. You would succeed if the suit breaks 3-3 or someone holds Q-x. You could try the same here – if nothing better comes to mind – but it cannot hurt to do some counting first.

You know that Steve had nine hearts and no clubs and he has turned up with one diamond. Moreover, if you believe the ◊J, you will put up him with the ◊Q. This accounts for 11 of his 13 cards, ruling out a 3-3 spade split. Even if Edgar meant the ◊J as a suit-preference signal or a false-card from K-Q-J, it remains more likely that diamonds are 7-2 rather than 8-1, again reducing the chance of an even spade division.

Of course, if West has the expected doubleton spade, it could include the queen. The odds, though, are against it. A better bet, once you see it, is to play him for 9-x or 10-x – slightly more chances. So, overtake the ♣J with the queen and lead the ♠J off dummy. If East covers, you win with the king, play a second round to the ace, picking up West's hoped-for nine or ten on the way and lead the eight for a ruffing finesse. You will be able to get back to dummy with a trump. East actually does better to duck the first spade. Then you run the jack, win the second spade in hand, lead the ♣3 to the five and ruff out the suit. You still have the ♣8 in dummy as a way to reach the long spade.

Give yourself a bonus point if you spotted and rejected (as it means giving up too much) a slim chance on a 5-1 spade break. If West has the bare ♠Q and East all the diamonds higher than the seven, you could squeeze East.

RESULTS ON BOARDS 1-8

Chris and Alex, who have been playing East-West in the closed room, arrive. 'We think we're quite good, but we might have missed a game, says Alex. 'Mind you, we defended one contract well', Chris adds.

On the tricky Board 1, when to make 5♣ you needed to find a trump coup, you will be pleased to hear you gained on the board even if you went down. Wayne and Sally stopped in 3NT. If someone miraculously had the ♣A-K bare and three hearts this might make, but Sally could take only seven tricks, giving your side 100. This means you pick up 11 IMPs if you made 5♣ or 2 IMPs if you went one down.

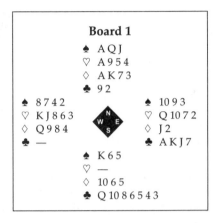

Board 1

	♠ A Q J	
	♡ A 9 5 4	
	◇ A K 7 3	
	♣ 9 2	
♠ 8 7 4 2		♠ 10 9 3
♡ K J 8 6 3		♡ Q 10 7 2
◇ Q 9 8 4		◇ J 2
♣ —		♣ A K J 7
	♠ K 6 5	
	♡ —	
	◇ 10 6 5	
	♣ Q 10 8 6 5 4 3	

On Board 2 Sally cautiously rebid 2◇ over 1NT. Wayne might have given false preference to 2♠, but he did not wish to keep the bidding open with only 6 points. 2◇ was not easy, but it made, giving Chris and Alex -90. So, if you flushed out the bare ♠A to make 4♠, you gain 11 IMPs. You lose 5 IMPs if you went one off and 7 if you went two off (overtaking the second club and losing three trumps as well).

On Board 3, the vulnerability deterred Chris from venturing 4♠. So, Alex had to lead after 1♡-3♠-4♡. Any suit except clubs might have been right. 4♡ makes on any lead, and Alex's choice of the ◇2 (into ◇K-J-9-x remember) gave declarer a shot at an overtrick, but not taken. You are thus plus 2 IMPs if you collected 500 but minus 6 if you only got 200.

West (Alex)
♠ K J
♡ K 9 8 4
◇ Q 10 7 2
♣ Q 8 3

On Board 4, Wayne decided he did not like any positive option with his 4-3-5-1 15-count over 3♡; even without his hesitation, Sally would hardly have reopened. The friendly lie of the cards gave your team 170 and 13 IMPs if you made 4♠ or still 2 IMPs if you went one down.

On Board 5, you were right that Chris would venture 3♠ on the 5-1-4-3 4-count Edgar passed after 1♡-Double-3♡, so team-mates sacrificed in 4♠ doubled, conceding 500 after losing two diamond ruffs. You therefore win 3 IMPs if you made 4♡ or lose 12 if you went down.

On Board 6, Alex cautiously bid only 1NT on the 3-3-4-3 10-count after the same 1♣ opening and 1♠ overcall (Steve jumped to 2NT you will recall). 1NT ended the auction. Sally as South played the ♠J at trick one, giving Chris and Alex an effortless 150. If you defeated 3NT, you gain 6 IMPs, whilst you lose 10 if you allowed nine tricks to make.

On Board 7, when to defeat 4♡ you had to exit with trump to avoid setting up a squeeze, events took a different turn in the other room. Wayne, North, even though he plays five-card majors, responded 1NT on his flat hand rather than raising to 2♠. East overcalled 2♡, South rebid 2♠, West raised to 3♡ and North competed to 3♠, which ended the auction. Your team mates did well to take this contract two off.

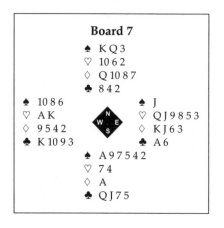

Board 7

♠ K Q 3
♡ 10 6 2
◇ Q 10 8 7
♣ 8 4 2

♠ 10 8 6   ♠ J
♡ A K   ♡ Q J 9 8 5 3
◇ 9 5 4 2   ◇ K J 6 3
♣ K 10 9 3   ♣ A 6

♠ A 9 7 5 4 2
♡ 7 4
◇ A
♣ Q J 7 5

What happened was that Alex cashed two top hearts and, reading Chris's ♡3 on the second round as a suit-preference signal for clubs, switched to the ♣3. Chris in turn worked out that such a low club lead (requesting a club return) must indicate the king. Accordingly, Chris took the ♣A, returned a club and scored a ruff. A third round of hearts then promoted West's 10-8-6 for a second undertrick. They reckon this made up for 'missing' 4♡. Their score of 200 means winning 7 IMPs if you defeated the heart game or losing 9 if you did not.

Board 8 generated less excitement at the other table. Wayne did not raise 5♣ to 6♣. Suffering the same heart ruff at trick one as you did, Sally settled for eleven top tricks and a score of 400. This means you win 11 IMPs if you made your slam or lose 10 if you went one down.

As expected, your captain, Chris, wants Pat and you to continue for the next set as North-South in the open room, with Phil and Sam going to the closed. The Director has just arrived to tell you that you will face the formidable (and still fresh) pair of Lucy and Suzanne. If you had any disasters on the first set, now is the time to put them out of mind.

BOARD 9   Dealer: North. E/W Vulnerable.

> **South (You)**
> ♠ Q 8 5 3
> ♡ K J 7 6 2
> ◇ 5
> ♣ A Q 5

Pat, the dealer, passes and Suzanne opens 1◇ in second seat. With a singleton in the suit opened and 5-4 in the majors, a take-out double stands out as the best action. Lucy responds 1NT and Pat bids 2♡. Suzanne rebids 2♠ and it your turn again. Although you have a fairly minimum double, it includes five-card support, giving justification for a raise to 3♡. Given Pat's free bid of 2♡ this might make and, at this vulnerability, you hardly care if 3♡ fails – the opponents can surely make a part-score somewhere. Suzanne reopens with 4◇ and, without sounding too enthusiastic about it, Lucy pushes on to 5◇.

West	North	East	South
Lucy	*Pat*	*Suzanne*	*You*
	Pass	1◇	Dbl
1NT	2♡	2♠	3♡
Pass	Pass	4◇	Pass
5◇	All Pass		

You lead the ♡6 and are sorry to see the ♣K in dummy.

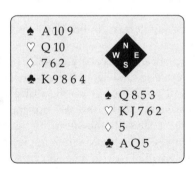

> ♠ A 10 9
> ♡ Q 10
> ◇ 7 6 2
> ♣ K 9 8 6 4
>
> ♠ Q 8 5 3
> ♡ K J 7 6 2
> ◇ 5
> ♣ A Q 5

Pat wins with the ♡A and returns the five. Suzanne dips into her bag for some pumpkin seeds and pops a few into her mouth. Then she ruffs with the ◇9, cashes the ◇A and leads the ♣2. How do you contend with this?

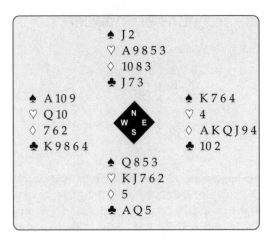

The bidding marks declarer with four spades and at least six diamonds, whilst the play to the first two tricks tells you she has a singleton heart.

At first sight it appears tempting to grab the ♣A in case the ♣2 is also a singleton, but a moment's reflection should enable you to work out that you have not much hope of beating the contract if East is 4-1-7-1. Suzanne must hold the missing kings because she would hardly have laid down the ◊A if missing the ◊K and Pat would surely have raised 3♡ to 4♡ with a 2-5-2-4 shape and 8 points, certainly if they are all working. This means you cannot safely attack spades and, after scoring the ♣A, you can do little better than return a club. Declarer will ruff, draw partner's last trump and still have the third round of diamonds and the ♠A as entries to set up the clubs. She will be able to discard one spade on the ♣K and another on the fifth club. In any case, with four spades to the king and seven running diamonds Suzanne would probably have bid 5◊ herself over 3♡. She is not known for holding back in the bidding.

To stand a realistic chance of success, you must place Suzanne with a 4-1-6-2 shape. This creates a new danger: the 3-3 club break with the ace onside leaves her well placed to set up the clubs. Clearly, you do not want to grab the ace and make the ♣K an entry. Do you see the importance of playing specifically the queen? If you duck, you will have to win the second round and be forced either to play a heart, which gives dummy an extra entry with a ruff, or a spade. True, you may survive by leading the ♠Q if Pat has the ♠J and declarer places you with this card, but why take a needless risk? If her other club is not the jack and you play the queen on the first round, partner can win the next club and exit safely with a trump (or, if dummy has no trumps left, a heart).

BOARD 10   Dealer: East. Game All.

> **South (You)**
> ♠ K J 10 8 5 3
> ♡ 8 4
> ♢ K J
> ♣ A K 3

'Diamonds are a girl's best friend' comes to mind when Suzanne again opens 1♢. Playing weak jump overcalls, you have an easy bid: 1♠ (to double and then bid spades would show more than you have). After a pass on your left, Pat bids 2♢, showing a value raise (it guarantees support as you play change-of-suit forcing) and Suzanne passes. You could mark time with 3♣ but a slam seems far away and often a direct approach pays dividends; your jump to 4♠ closes the auction.

West	North	East	South
Lucy	*Pat*	*Suzanne*	*You*
		1♢	1♠
Pass	2♢	Pass	4♠
All Pass			

Lucy, West, leads the ♢2 and, at first, all seems well.

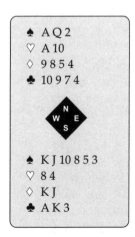

> ♠ A Q 2
> ♡ A 10
> ♢ 9 8 5 4
> ♣ 10 9 7 4
>
> ♠ K J 10 8 5 3
> ♡ 8 4
> ♢ K J
> ♣ A K 3

Unfortunately, Suzanne wins with the ace and returns the ♢7, which Lucy ruffs. After adjusting her glasses, which had fallen slightly down her nose, she switches to the ♡Q. What is your plan?

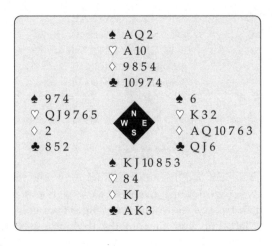

With two tricks already lost and a heart loser exposed, you must avoid losing a club. You can do this if West has 8-x, a bare eight, queen or jack or if anyone has Q-J bare. Of course, none of these layouts seems very likely. Might an indirect method to avoid the club loser succeed?

A squeeze on East will not work even if she has sole guard in clubs because dummy has no late entry. Nor will ruffing two diamonds in hand, drawing trumps, cashing the top clubs and exiting with a heart work. West's switch to the ♡Q tells you the defenders can choose who wins the heart. So, however the black suits lie, nobody will have to give you a ruff a discard. One idea for an endplay that might work is to cash only one top club. If East has a bare ♣Q or ♣J, and you can strip the spades and diamonds, whoever wins the second heart will be stuck.

The right line is to take the ♡A, ruff a diamond high, cross to dummy with a trump and ruff the last diamond high. Then play a second trump to dummy to leave the position shown. It would be wrong now to lead a heart. As dummy lacks an entry, the defenders can exit in clubs. Instead, lead the ♣10, forcing East to cover, and only then play a heart. You may also succeed if East is 1-2-6-4 with ♣Q-J-8-x. If she has kept the ♡K, she must win a heart exit;

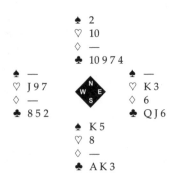

if not, you might cash a second club hoping to endplay West. 'Not much we can do about that,' Suzanne will remark if you made the contract.

BOARD 11   Dealer: South. Love All.

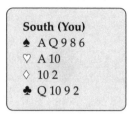

South (You)
♠ A Q 9 8 6
♡ A 10
♢ 10 2
♣ Q 10 9 2

You open 1♠, Lucy doubles and Pat raises to 3♠. This shows four- or maybe five-card support and a hand that would normally raise to 2♠. Suzanne tries 3NT, and you have another bid. If you think 3NT will make, you can sacrifice in 4♠, hoping to lose at most 300. With this hand, though, you feel quite optimistic. With the ♡A entry, you picture scoring four spades and a heart. Moreover, if declarer needs to play on clubs or Pat has a winner, 3NT might go two down. If so, then knowing Suzanne bids aggressively, perhaps you should double. Go for it!

West	North	East	South
Lucy	Pat	Suzanne	You
			1♠
Dbl	3♠	3NT	Dbl
All Pass			

You lead the ♣8, and this goes ten, five, seven. The running diamonds on view tell you what is coming next.

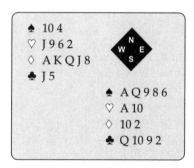

♠ 10 4
♡ J 9 6 2
♢ A K Q J 8
♣ J 5

♠ A Q 9 8 6
♡ A 10
♢ 10 2
♣ Q 10 9 2

Pat follows with the ♢3 (low from an odd number), then the seven and six. Declarer also follows to three rounds, and you pitch the ♣10. On the fourth round, Pat throws the ♡3 (discouraging) and East the ♣3. You must find two more discards, one now and one on the fifth round.

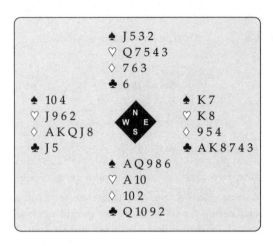

Pat's ◊7 on the second diamond should be a suit-preference signal, here denying club values. If you are right, declarer has eight tricks ready to run: five diamonds, two clubs and a spade. From Pat's low heart discard, you can also put Suzanne with the ♡K. This places you in some difficulty.

If you throw another club on the fourth or fifth round of diamonds, you will allow declarer to make all the rest of her clubs and probably make an overtrick or two. You therefore exclude this possibility. You do not want to release a heart either. If Suzanne reads the position, and your double has probably made it easier for her to do so, she can duck a heart to flush out your ace. Lump it or like it, you will have to part with two spades, and let us suppose you part with the ♣6 first.

On the fifth round, you must retain the ♠A as declarer still has the king. A little thought makes it clear that the card to throw is the ♠Q. If you leave yourself without a link to Pat's hand, you will be thrown in and forced to make a losing lead. Now if declarer leads a spade to your ace, you have a choice of plays. You can either play the ♠9 to partner's two winners and, if declarer keeps two clubs and two

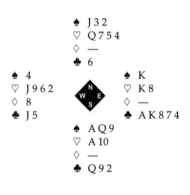

hearts, wait for Pat to throw her in to lead a heart. Alternatively, you can exit with a flamboyant ♣Q. 'Not much we could do about that either,' Suzanne will observe as she returns her cards to the board if you made this one too.

Win the Big Match

Dealer: West. N/S Vulnerable.

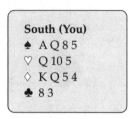

South (You)
♠ A Q 8 5
♡ Q 10 5
◇ K Q 5 4
♣ 8 3

Lucy, on your left, opens 1♠, Pat doubles and Suzanne passes. What should you do? With a flat hand and a double stopper in opener's suit, 3NT seems tempting. As against that, even a near minimum opposite could give a slam great play. For example, Pat could hold a singleton spade, ♡A-J-9-x, ace to five diamonds and ace to three clubs. To express a doubt about whether 3NT is the right contract, you start with a 2♠ cue-bid. If nothing exciting happens, you can bid 3NT next time...

West	North	East	South
Lucy	*Pat*	*Suzanne*	*You*
1♠	Dbl	Pass	2♠
Pass	3♣	Pass	3NT
All Pass			

West leads the ♠6 and, after dummy comes down, you allow yourself a rueful smile. A slam stands no chance facing this North hand!

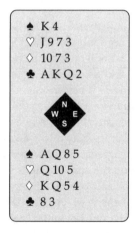

♠ K 4
♡ J 9 7 3
◇ 10 7 3
♣ A K Q 2

♠ A Q 8 5
♡ Q 10 5
◇ K Q 5 4
♣ 8 3

How can you meet the modest target of nine tricks?

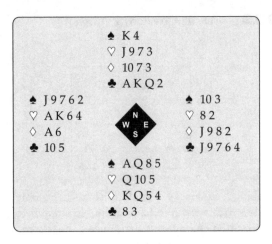

```
              ♠ K 4
              ♡ J 9 7 3
              ◇ 10 7 3
              ♣ A K Q 2
♠ J 9 7 6 2                    ♠ 10 3
♡ A K 6 4         N            ♡ 8 2
◇ A 6         W       E        ◇ J 9 8 2
♣ 10 5           S            ♣ J 9 7 6 4
              ♠ A Q 8 5
              ♡ Q 10 5
              ◇ K Q 5 4
              ♣ 8 3
```

You count six top winners in the black suits and spot the potential to develop three more in the reds, two hearts and a diamond. Since you have the potential to arrive at the nine tricks required, you turn your mind to the danger of losing five tricks first.

Lucy and Suzanne can open a four-card major, but only on a hand too strong for a weak no-trump and with a decent suit. So you know Lucy has at least five spades. The lack of values missing means that, unless she has something like a 5-5, she will also hold the two big hearts and the ◇A. So, if you follow straightforward lines, you will go down. If you win the first trick with the ♠Q and, say, play a heart, Lucy will win and lead a second spade, knocking out dummy's king. You are then down to one stopper but Lucy still has two aces left as entries.

It would not help to play diamonds before hearts. Even if the ◇J drops doubleton, you will still need a heart trick. One idea is to duck the first trick. If spades are 6-1, East will switch, presumably to a diamond; then you will probably duck and be safe if East has the jack. This idea has merit, but I hope you can see a better one. Assuming Lucy would lead the jack from J-10-9, running the lead to your hand serves no purpose. Instead, win the first trick in dummy. Now when West gets in with a heart she can do better than to play a low spade, and you allow East to win the trick. After eating a few more pumpkin seeds, Suzanne shifts to a diamond and, unless you think its size tells you that West has the jack, you duck. You may not be able to make the contract if Lucy has ◇A-J-x, and her spade length and top cards in the red suits leave far more room for Suzanne to hold the ◇J anyway. As the cards lie, you cannot afford to put up the king, as Lucy could win, return a diamond and hold up her second heart winner to leave you a trick short.

BOARD 13   Dealer: North. Game All.

South (You)
- ♠ K Q 9 8 7 6
- ♡ K 5 3
- ◇ A 6
- ♣ 7 2

Pat, North, opens 1♣ and East, passes. You respond 1♠ and Lucy bids 2NT – the unusual no-trump, showing the other two suits. Pat passes and Lucy bids 3◇. It seems unclear whether 3♠ from you is forcing now, but you hardly care. Pat knows the value of a vulnerable game and will strain to bid again. Indeed a raise to 4♠ is what you get.

West	North	East	South
Lucy	*Pat*	*Suzanne*	*You*
	1♣	Pass	1♠
2NT	Pass	3◇	3♠
Pass	4♠	All Pass	

West leads the ◇7 and you see why Pat did not bid 3♠ over 2NT. For an immediate raise you would have expected something better than a balanced eight-loser hand. Presumably Pat intended to reopen with 3♠ if you had passed over 3◇, and this seems a sensible approach.

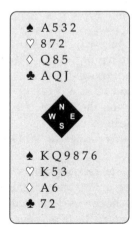

- ♠ A 5 3 2
- ♡ 8 7 2
- ◇ Q 8 5
- ♣ A Q J

- ♠ K Q 9 8 7 6
- ♡ K 5 3
- ◇ A 6
- ♣ 7 2

Of course, bidding well is one thing. Now can you make the contract?

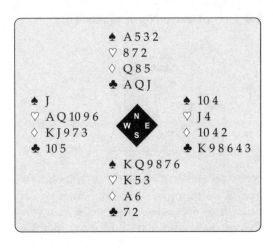

You cannot succeed if every card sits wrong, but this seems unlikely. Lucy would not lead the ◇7 from J-10-9-7-x, so you expect to find the ◇K onside and score a trick with dummy's queen. Sadly, even if you score the ◇Q at trick one, you face another hurdle. With length in the red suits on the left, hence club length on the right, you must fear that West has the ♡A over your king and East the ♣K over dummy's holding. If you take a losing club finesse and East has two hearts other than precisely 6-4, you will lose three heart tricks and the contract.

The solution comes with avoidance play. You must arrange to lose a trick in diamonds rather than clubs, discarding a club on a diamond. This will enable you to take a ruffing club finesse and keep East out. It is no good, though, winning the first two diamonds and losing the third to East's ten. You must force West to win by playing the eight at trick one and capturing the

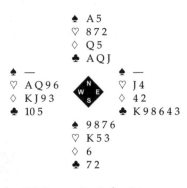

ten with the ace. Then, having cashed the ♠K-Q, you lead the ◇6.

If Lucy wins with the king, she can switch to a club. In this case you put up the ace, discard a club on the ◇Q and run the ♣Q, not caring whether it wins or loses. If, instead, she covers the six with the nine, you win with the queen in dummy and return the five, again getting rid of a club. You now appreciate the importance of playing dummy's eight at trick one. If you had not forced out Suzanne's ten, Lucy could certainly beat you by playing the jack on the second round of diamonds.

                 Win the Big Match

BOARD 14   Dealer: East. Love All.

```
              South (You)
              ♠ Q 9 6
              ♡ A 10 7 4 3
              ◇ 9 5 3
              ♣ A 2
```

Suzanne on your right opens 2♠. Non-vulnerable she hardly promises a good suit, but you do expect a six-carder. Two passes follow and Pat reopens with a double. You have more than the 8 points partner might expect and a five-card suit to boot. This entitles you to make a non-minimum response. Thoughts of 3NT may flit through your mind as the ♠Q may count for little in 4♡, but you dismiss them.

West	North	East	South
Lucy	*Pat*	*Suzanne*	*You*
		2♠	Pass
Pass	Dbl	Pass	4♡
All Pass			

After neatly inscribing the contract on her score-card, Lucy leads the ♠A, and Pat lays out the dummy.

```
♠ K 2
♡ J 9 6 2
◇ K Q 6
♣ K Q 7 3

        N
      W   E
        S

♠ Q 9 6
♡ A 10 7 4 3
◇ 9 5 3
♣ A 2
```

East follows with the ♠7 and West switches to the ◇J. You call for the king, but East produces the ace and returns the eight. You win this second round of diamonds in dummy and consider your prospects.

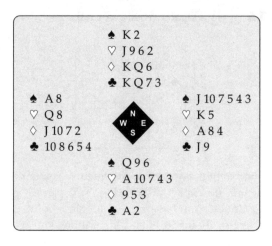

```
              ♠ K 2
              ♡ J 9 6 2
              ◊ K Q 6
              ♣ K Q 7 3
♠ A 8                        ♠ J 10 7 5 4 3
♡ Q 8            N           ♡ K 5
◊ J 10 7 2     W   E         ◊ A 8 4
♣ 10 8 6 5 4     S           ♣ J 9
              ♠ Q 9 6
              ♡ A 10 7 4 3
              ◊ 9 5 3
              ♣ A 2
```

If you play without any particular plan, you will go down. For example, if you take a trump finesse and West wins, the defenders will then cash a diamond, which will be the setting trick.

Rather than taking a trump finesse, perhaps you should play a trump to the ace. Indeed if East has ♡K-8-5 or ♡Q-8-5, she may well have only two diamonds and this strategy will keep your trump losers to one and keep West off play. A chance also exists that East may hold ♡K-x and fail to unblock. In this case, if she has only two diamonds, again you can make the contract. The trouble with this is that you have no reason to expect a 5-2 diamond split. Suzanne's return of the ◊8, the highest diamond she could have left, is consistent with a three-card holding.

At the risk of a ruff, you do best to try getting rid of a diamond before broaching trumps. Knowing that West can surely ruff the third spade, whilst three clubs might stand up, it looks tempting to play on clubs. Watch what happens if you do. Knowing the ♡K has little value unless her partner holds the ♡Q, East ruffs the third club high. Whether you overruff and try the spades, or pitch a diamond, you finish one down.

It is a different story if you start with the ♠K. (You are sure West has another spade, or they would presumably have taken a ruff already; also, with a seven-card suit, albeit only jack high, Suzanne would have opened 3♠ at this vulnerability). Next you cross to the ♣A and advance the ♠Q. If West ruffs with the queen, dummy discards the ◊6 and you can hope that a later finesse against the ♡K will land the contract. If West ruffs low, dummy overruffs and you draw a round of trumps with the ace. When all follow, you play two more high clubs, just needing the first of these not to be ruffed for you to discard your diamond loser.

```
South (You)
♠ A 8 3 2
♡ K 5
◇ 9 7 5 3
♣ A 9 5
```

You deal and pass. Although you have excellent controls, you lack the playing strength to open the bidding. Lucy opens 1◇, Pat doubles and Suzanne passes. What should you do?

A jump to 2♠ shows at least four spades and 8-10 points, maybe a poor 11. Given that you could hardly have a better hand having passed first time, this seems an underbid. 3♠ expresses the values better, but sounds unattractive on a four-card suit. A 2◇ cue-bid must be best. Pat rebids 2♡, you introduce the spades and Pat puts you to game.

West	North	East	South
Lucy	Pat	Suzanne	You
			Pass
1◇	Dbl	Pass	2◇
Pass	2♡	Pass	2♠
Pass	4♠	All Pass	

Lucy rearranges her cards a couple of times and then leads the ♠5. How you do plan the play?

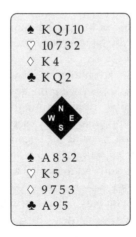

```
♠ K Q J 10
♡ 10 7 3 2
◇ K 4
♣ K Q 2

         N
       W   E
         S

♠ A 8 3 2
♡ K 5
◇ 9 7 5 3
♣ A 9 5
```

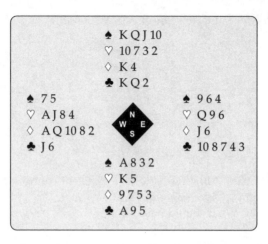

                    ♠ K Q J 10
                    ♡ 10 7 3 2
                    ◊ K 4
                    ♣ K Q 2
    ♠ 7 5   ♠ 9 6 4
    ♡ A J 8 4   ♡ Q 9 6
    ◊ A Q 10 8 2   N   ◊ J 6
    ♣ J 6   W   E   ♣ 10 8 7 4 3
                      S
                    ♠ A 8 3 2
                    ♡ K 5
                    ◊ 9 7 5 3
                    ♣ A 9 5

You can count eight tricks: four spades, three clubs and, assuming Lucy holds the ◊A for her opening bid (and failure to lead the suit), one in diamonds. This means that unless Suzanne unexpectedly turns up with the ♡A you will need two ruffs to bring the total to ten.

For two reasons, it looks appealing to go for heart ruffs rather than for diamond ruffs. For one thing, if trumps break 4-1, you can ill afford to ruff high twice. For another, the lack of entries to your hand will make the timing difficult, especially as you have to use one entry to lead a diamond to the king. How then should you set about these ruffs?

Anticipating a problem often puts you halfway or more towards solving it. Here you can foresee the danger ahead. Suppose you win the first trump in dummy and play a heart to the king. West will win with the ace and play a second trump. Then, unless the defender who has run out of trumps has both the queen and jack of hearts, one or other opponent will be able to play a third round of trumps. Obviously, you cannot make two ruffs in one hand if you only have left one trump in each.

Knowing that the ♡A almost certainly sits offside, you should budget for two heart losers and focus on reducing the ability of your opponents to play a third round of trumps. After winning the trump in dummy, duck a heart! Either defender can win and play a second round of trumps but, after getting in with the ♡A, West, if she began with a doubleton trump, will be unable to play a third round. Provided you do not encounter any foul breaks in the minors, you can then play a diamond to the king and take two heart ruffs in peace; you may even survive a 4-1 trump split. If you found the right play, you may notice a philosophical nod from Lucy as she returns her cards to the board.

BOARD 16   Dealer: West. E/W Vulnerable.

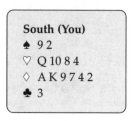

> **South (You)**
> ♠ 9 2
> ♡ Q 10 8 4
> ◇ A K 9 7 4 2
> ♣ 3

You are fourth to speak – or should I say to pull a card out of a bidding box! Lucy opens 1♣, natural in their system, and Pat overcalls 2♡, weak. Not to be outdone, Suzanne also makes a 'stop' bid: 4♣. (In any form of duplicate you forewarn your opponents of a jump bid by saying 'stop' or, if bidding boxes are in use, by displaying the appropriate card). With four-card support, you have no intention of selling out.

Raising to 4♡ is clearly one option, but this bid does nothing to help partner, either in judging whether to compete to the five level or, if you end up defending a club contract, with the lead. You therefore bid 4◇. Lucy seems scarcely troubled by this development and cue bids 4♡. Suzanne hastily signs off in 5♣ to leave this as the complete auction:

West	North	East	South
Lucy	*Pat*	*Suzanne*	*You*
1♣	2♡	4♣	4◇
4♡	Pass	5♣	All Pass

Pat leads the ◇Q and dummy comes down on your right. 'Thank you, partner,' Lucy intones as if she was greeting a class.

> ♠ Q 8 5 4
> ♡ —
> ◇ 10 8 3
> ♣ K Q 10 8 4 2
>
> ♠ 9 2
> ♡ Q 10 8 4
> ◇ A K 9 7 4 2
> ♣ 3

How can you expect to score three tricks?

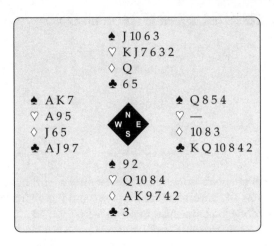

Lucy would hardly cue-bid 4♡ looking for a slam on a jack-high trump suit. So, you can dismiss any thought of a trump trick. If you are to beat this game, you will need two diamonds and one spade, one diamond and two spades or, with the aid of a ruff, three diamonds.

Scoring two spade tricks appears unlikely, partly for the reason we discussed before. With nothing in diamonds, Lucy needs good spades to justify her slam try. This reduces your winning options to two.

If declarer has a doubleton diamond, there is probably no need to do anything special. You can cash two diamonds and, if partner has a spade winner, it can hardly run away. If the ◊Q wins the first trick, Pat will be able to work out that a diamond continuation is safe and even an unlikely lead from ♠K-x-x-x should not cause too much harm.

If, however, declarer has three diamonds, you may need to take care. If you let the ◊Q win, Pat will have to switch at trick two; a danger then exists that declarer has the ♡A as a parking place for one of dummy's diamonds and ♠A-K-x to solidify the spade position. To cater for this situation, you should overtake the ◊Q with the king and follow with the ace. When partner shows out, a ruff seals the contract's fate. Just about the only time that playing three rounds of diamonds can cost is if West has ◊J-x, ♠A-x and all six missing trumps. This would leave Pat with 5-6 in the majors, which would make the 2♡ call very odd.

If you manage to win the first three tricks, this will curtail the play as Lucy can claim one down at trick four. This means you finish a few minutes before your team-mates and can relax ... momentarily.

RESULTS ON BOARDS 9·16

'A bit up and down', says Sam coming in with Phil to join you, 'we had some good ones but I made one unlucky opening lead and they found a fine endplay.' Phil, sounding slightly more positive, adds: 'Yes, they took a phantom sacrifice and I loved making 3NT on a strip squeeze.'

On Board 9, the bidding started the same way but Sam decided against going on to 5◊. The ♡Q and ♣K were dubious values facing 6-4 in the other two suits. With the success of a 4◊ contract not in doubt, the defenders dropped a trick, giving East-West 150. So, you gain 6 IMPs if you created a club entry to partner to beat the game. You lose 10 if you failed to do so.

West (Sam)
♠ A 10 9
♡ Q 10
◊ 7 6 2
♣ K 9 8 6 4

On Board 10 Steve and Edgar as North-South also bid to 4♠ and your team-mates found the diamond ruff. Unfortunately, Steve timed the play perfectly, creating the frozen club suit before exiting with a heart. If you did the same, you flatten the board. If not, mark down 12 IMPs away.

On Board 11, Phil played in 3NT undoubled. Steve led the same as you, the ♠8, and Phil also put up dummy's ten. Failing to work out that Steve would lead the king from K-Q-9-8 on this bidding, however, Edgar covered with the jack. This left Steve with no means of getting off lead in the end-game and, by reading the position correctly, Phil brought home the game. So, you win 12 IMPs if you beat 3NT doubled and lose only 4 if you did not.

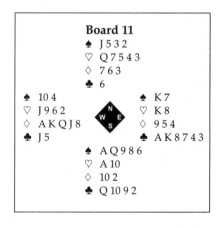

Board 11
♠ J 5 3 2
♡ Q 7 5 4 3
◊ 7 6 3
♣ 6

♠ 10 4   ♠ K 7
♡ J 9 6 2   ♡ K 8
◊ A K Q J 8   ◊ 9 5 4
♣ J 5   ♣ A K 8 7 4 3

♠ A Q 9 8 6
♡ A 10
◊ 10 2
♣ Q 10 9 2

On Board 12, Steve blasted 3NT in response to the take-out double on your hand. Sam considered which major suit to lead from ♣J-9-x-x-x and ♡A-K-x-x. Alas, thinking more about the weak spades than the bounty of entries, Sam chose a top heart, giving declarer an easy ride. So, if you made 3NT, the board is flat. If you went down, you lose 11 IMPs.

On Board 13, the bidding began the same way: 1♣-Pass-1♠ and a 2NT overcall. Then Edgar went for the simple if undisciplined action of raising South's spades immediately. On this sequence, Phil had not shown preference for diamonds, so there was less reason to lead the suit. Sam chose the ♣10 and the declarer finessed, giving Phil the losing option of trying for a club ruff. Fortunately, Phil did not fancy it and a heart switch gave them the first four tricks.

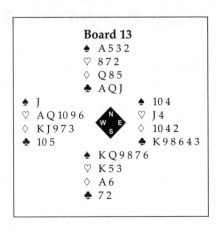

Board 13
```
                ♠ A 5 3 2
                ♡ 8 7 2
                ◇ Q 8 5
                ♣ A Q J
  ♠ J                         ♠ 10 4
  ♡ A Q 10 9 6                ♡ J 4
  ◇ K J 9 7 3                 ◇ 10 4 2
  ♣ 10 5                      ♣ K 9 8 6 4 3
                ♠ K Q 9 8 7 6
                ♡ K 5 3
                ◇ A 6
                ♣ 7 2
```

The upshot is that you gain 12 IMPs if you found the key diamond play to make 4♠. Missing it and going one down produces a flat board.

On Board 14 Phil decided against opening 2♠ on J-10-x-x-x-x and Edgar opened 1♣ in fourth seat. Phil overcalled 1♠, Steve with your hand bid 2♡, and Edgar's raise to 3♡ ended the auction. Sam led the ♠A but did not find the diamond switch and ten tricks resulted. This means you win or lose 6 IMPs depending on whether you made 4♡.

Steve did not bid as well as you on Board 15. After the same start to the auction, Pass-1◇-Double-Pass, he tried a simple 2♠. With no aces and facing a passed hand, Edgar reasonably thought he did not have enough to raise, and 2♠ became the final contract. Perhaps this was as well, for Steve made only nine tricks after the same trump lead as you had. You gain 10 IMPs if you made 4♠ or lose 6 if you went off.

At the other table there was more action on Board 16. Whilst you and Pat sold out to 5♣, Steve and Edgar sacrificed in 5♡ doubled, going down 300. This gives you the chance to win 9 IMPs if you took the first three tricks against 5♣. Should you have let it through, you lose 7.

If, contrary to expectations, Chris has decided to rotate the three pairs in your team, you would find out now, as it would be your turn to miss a set. No – Chris says you must be playing too well for a rest! For the opponents, Steve and Edgar will sit out, so you and Pat will return to your seats to take on Wayne and Sally.

BOARD 17   Dealer: North. Love All.

> **South (You)**
> ♠ A K Q 10 9 4
> ♡ 8 5
> ◇ Q 7 4
> ♣ K 6

In third seat, you open 1♠ and Wayne, on your left, bids 2♠. This is a Michaels cue-bid, showing hearts and a minor with at least five cards in each. Pat doubles, promising values (akin to a redouble of a take-out double). Sally passes, as do you. Wayne retreats to 3◇, Sally gives preference to 3♡ and it is your turn to bid. Arguably, 3♠ should be forcing (you would act earlier with weakness) but you take no chances.

West	North	East	South
Wayne	*Pat*	*Sally*	*You*
	Pass	Pass	1♠
2♠	Dbl	Pass	Pass
3◇	Pass	3♡	4♠
All Pass			

West starts with the ♡K (not denying the ace) and you see dummy.

> ♠ J 2
> ♡ J 10 3
> ◇ A 6 3
> ♣ A 8 7 3 2
>
> ♠ A K Q 10 9 4
> ♡ 8 5
> ◇ Q 7 4
> ♣ K 6

After fine-tuning the angle on his cap, Wayne continues with the queen and ace of hearts, East following with the two, then the four and nine. How do you proceed from here?

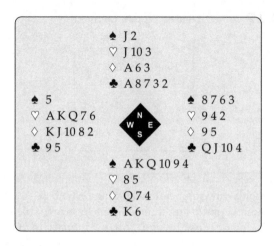

Counting nine top tricks, you see two possibilities of making a tenth: the ◇Q and a long club.

Chances of winning a trick with the ◇Q seem poor. Sally's decision to play the lower of her two remaining hearts, the four, on the second round of hearts looks like a suit-preference signal for clubs. In any event, if Wayne has five diamonds to Sally's two, he figures to hold the king. Endplay chances appear equally slim. You would need to find West with a singleton trump and precisely K-J-10-9-8 in diamonds; then you could draw one trump, cash the two top clubs and duck a diamond.

Realistically you need to aim for a long club. Two ruffs will set up the clubs easily enough if they split no worse than 4-2 and trumps are 3-2. Unfortunately, if Wayne has 10 cards in the red suits, he cannot hold a doubleton in each black suit. This means that irrespective of whether he has a 1-5-5-2 or 0-5-5-3 shape you will have too few trumps to ruff a heart, ruff a club or two and draw East's trumps. Nor is it likely to help to discard on the third round of clubs, trying to conserve your trumps. Sally will win and switch to a diamond, taking out dummy's late entry.

The way to keep everything under control is beautifully simple: do not ruff the third round of hearts but discard a diamond instead! If, as you suspect from Wayne's bidding and Sally's carding, Wayne holds the ◇K, he will be unable to knock out dummy's ◇A entry. On a trump switch, you win in hand, play the king, ace and a third club. You ruff this high and, when West shows out, continue with a trump to the jack and a second club ruff. Then you draw the remaining trumps and cross to the ◇A to enjoy the last club.

BOARD 18   Dealer: East. N/S Vulnerable.

> **South (You)**
> ♠ 10 9 3
> ♡ A K 3
> ◇ A K Q 3
> ♣ K J 7

Sally on your right opens 1♣ (better minor). Clearly, you have too much for a 1NT overcall and start with a double. Wayne passes and Pat bids 1♡. You have 20 points, but this should not cause you to get overly excited. If 1NT on the previous round would have shown 15 up to 17 or a poor 18, 1NT now should show a good 18 up to 20. Pat, who must be upper range for the earlier 1♡ bid, raises to 3NT.

West	North	East	South
Wayne	*Pat*	*Sally*	*You*
		1♣	Dbl
Pass	1♡	Pass	1NT
Pass	3NT	All Pass	

Wayne offers everyone a peppermint before popping one himself and leading the ♠7 (presumably top of nothing). This comes as no surprise as Wayne and Sally often open 1♣ (or 1◇) on a flat 12-14.

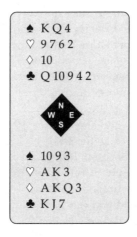

> ♠ K Q 4
> ♡ 9 7 6 2
> ◇ 10
> ♣ Q 10 9 4 2
>
> ♠ 10 9 3
> ♡ A K 3
> ◇ A K Q 3
> ♣ K J 7

You play the king from dummy and East encourages with eight. How do you handle the play?

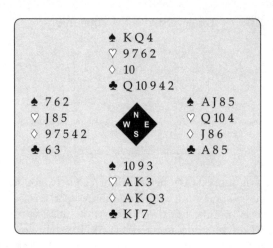

The opening lead is annoying, as it has removed dummy's only entry outside clubs. Sally is no fool and knows to hold up the ace of clubs to restrict the tricks you can make in the suit. Moreover, since they play 'better minor', i.e. they open 1◊ with three diamonds and two clubs, you know that she has at least ace to three clubs.

Your general plan must be an elimination play so that when Sally does take her ♣A she will only have black cards left and be compelled to concede an entry to dummy. You can achieve this easily enough if she has no more than two hearts and three diamonds – simply by cashing winners. However, it seems perfectly possible that Sally has a 4-3-3-3 distribution. Then, unless she holds precisely Q-J-10 of hearts, she can unblock to leave West with the third-round winner. To prevent this from happening, you must lead hearts twice from dummy, ducking if she plays the queen. Entries are short, so lead a heart at trick two.

Assuming East plays low, you win, cross to the ♣9 (or play the ♣J to the ♣Q) and lead a second heart. Sally does best to play the ♡Q and she can exit with a heart. You can take the ♣K next (this would be essential if East were 4-4-2-3) and then play off your top diamonds. Sally can unblock the ◊J but it does her no good and this is the position at trick nine. Dummy can throw a club or the master heart on the ◊Q and East is stuck when you lead a club next.

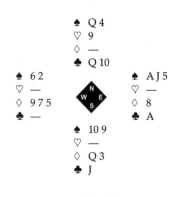

BOARD 19   Dealer: South. E/W Vulnerable.

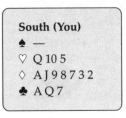

South (You)
♠ —
♡ Q 10 5
◇ A J 9 8 7 3 2
♣ A Q 7

You open 1◇ and, after two passes, Sally on your right reopens with a double. With a weaker hand this shape you would have pre-empted 3◇ initially, so why not do so now? On average partner will hold two diamonds, giving your side a nine-card fit and safety, especially at this vulnerability, at the three level. (With the Law of Total Tricks, if the high cards are evenly spread, you should make eight tricks if each side has an eight-card fit, nine tricks with a nine-card fit and so on). Again, two passes and a double follow your bid. Having shot your bolt, you pass this time. Wayne bids 3♠ and Sally, after giving the matter just a little thought, raises to 4♠. This makes the complete auction as follows:

West	North	East	South
Wayne	*Pat*	*Sally*	*You*
			1◇
Pass	Pass	Dbl	3◇
Pass	Pass	Dbl	Pass
3♠	Pass	4♠	All Pass

Pat leads the ◇10 and dummy comes down on your right. 'Thank you, sweetheart,' Wayne says, 'very nice.'

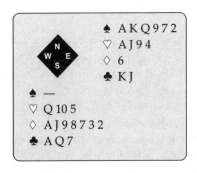

```
                    ♠ A K Q 9 7 2
           N        ♡ A J 9 4
        W     E     ◇ 6
           S        ♣ K J

  ♠ —
  ♡ Q 10 5
  ◇ A J 9 8 7 3 2
  ♣ A Q 7
```

How do you plan to take four defensive tricks?

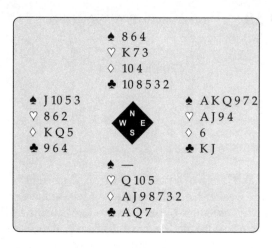

It seems most unlikely that Wayne would have bid 3♠ on three low spades when he could have passed for penalties. Therefore, you must aim to score four tricks in the side suits. If you put Pat with the ♡K, as I think you must, you can actually envisage five tricks: two hearts, two clubs and a diamond. The snag, of course, arises with the diamond position.

Since you can see the ◊9 in your hand, the lead must be from 10-x or a singleton. If you instinctively play 'third hand high' and put up the ◊A, you will establish the king-queen in declarer's hand for discards. True, he may not have an easy entry to them if Pat has ♠J-x-x, but there is little hope of defeating the contract if you part with the ◊A at trick one. You count nine tricks for declarer – six trumps, two diamonds and the ♡A. In addition, he can either score a long heart (if he has three hearts) or a ruff (if he has a doubleton). Remember, if you win the first trick then you are going to have to lead something, presumably a heart. This will allow declarer to set up any heart ruff without losing the lead to Pat by using dummy's ace to capture the king.

Sacrificing your diamond trick, by ducking the first round of the suit, does not take you not completely out of the woods. Declarer may draw a round of trumps with the jack, on which you can certainly spare a diamond, and play a club to the jack. In this case, you have a choice of exits after winning this with the ♣Q: either lead the ♡5, or cash the ♣A and then, in case West has the ♣10, play either the ♡5 or a club. More dangerous perhaps is if Wayne leaves clubs alone and plays a heart to the nine. Now, having got in with the ♡10, you have only one card to lead that will both avoid setting up a trick and protect you from an endplay later: the ♡Q.

Win the Big Match

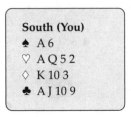

```
South (You)
♠ A 6
♡ A Q 5 2
◇ K 10 3
♣ A J 10 9
```

Wayne deals and opens 3◇. Pat, slightly to your surprise, overcalls 3♡. Sally, rather less to your surprise, passes. You could cue-bid 4◇ (your methods allow a second-round control at the four level or lower, especially here), but one finds it hard to see how this can help. So, you jump to 4NT. Pat responds 5◇, which, in the traditional method of Roman Key Card Blackwood, shows either an ace or the ♡K. (Hearts are agreed by inference and Pat cannot have four key cards when you hold three). Since you might lose the first two tricks in a heart slam on a diamond lead and you have enough values to hope for twelve tricks without doing any ruffing, you jump to 6NT.

West	North	East	South
Wayne	*Pat*	*Sally*	*You*
3◇	3♡	Pass	4NT
Pass	5◇	Pass	6NT
All Pass			

West leads the ♠9 and dummy's ♠Q holds. Can you make your slam?

```
♠ Q J 8
♡ K 10 9 8 7 3
◇ J 6
♣ K 6
```

```
♠ A 6
♡ A Q 5 2
◇ K 10 3
♣ A J 10 9
```

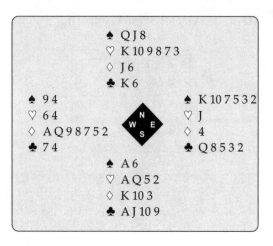

          ♠ Q J 8
          ♡ K 10 9 8 7 3
          ◇ J 6
          ♣ K 6
♠ 9 4   ♠ K 10 7 5 3 2
♡ 6 4   ♡ J
◇ A Q 9 8 7 5 2   ◇ 4
♣ 7 4   ♣ Q 8 5 3 2
          ♠ A 6
          ♡ A Q 5 2
          ◇ K 10 3
          ♣ A J 10 9

The opening lead has spared you any worries about the spade suit and given you ten tricks on top. You still need two more.

If East has the bare ◇Q, that will do it, but this seems most unlikely. Wayne is vulnerable, and he could have opened 2◇, weak, so surely holds A-Q to seven. Therefore, you need to do something with clubs. If the queen lies with the defender holding fewer clubs (almost certainly West), you can take one finesse and subsequently wait for the queen to fall under the king and ace. Of course, rather more often, the ♣Q will be with the length and this plan will fail.

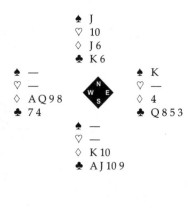

You start by cashing two hearts to get a count on West's hand. When he follows twice, you know that East has the long clubs. Next you unblock the ♠A, and finish the hearts. To keep the ♠K and ♣Q adequately guarded after the last of these, Sally has to part with her exit card, the ◇4, and you throw a diamond as well. Finally, you play a club to the jack, praying that it wins. When it does, you cross to the ♣K and exit with a spade.

Note that from this position no ambiguity arises, but Sally could have kept two spades and three clubs. You could then pick up the ♣Q, but if you read her as 5-1-1-6 (less likely, as the ♠9 is not obvious from 9-x-x and there are fewer clubs missing), she would make two spade tricks.

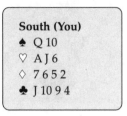

South (You)
♠ Q 10
♡ A J 6
◇ 7 6 5 2
♣ J 10 9 4

Pat, North, opens 1◇ and East, passes. Playing inverted raises (where 2◇ is strong), a raise is out as you would not want to bid 3◇ with poor trumps. A 1♡ response may lead to big problems and a pass makes it too easy for West to bid, so you try 1NT. Pat reverses to 2♠, which is forcing. You take the opportunity to express your diamond support and, when Pat continues with 3♡, you close proceedings with 3NT.

West	North	East	South
Wayne	*Pat*	*Sally*	*You*
	1◇	Pass	1NT
Pass	2♠	Pass	3◇
Pass	3♡	Pass	3NT
All Pass			

West leads the ♣5 and dummy has the expected 4-3-5-1 pattern.

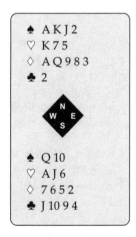

♠ A K J 2
♡ K 7 5
◇ A Q 9 8 3
♣ 2

♠ Q 10
♡ A J 6
◇ 7 6 5 2
♣ J 10 9 4

East wins the first trick with the king and returns the seven. Your jack holds as West follows with the three. How do you continue?

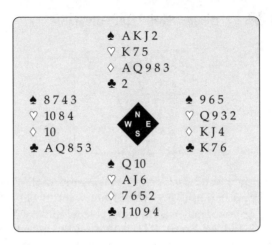

```
              ♠ A K J 2
              ♡ K 7 5
              ◇ A Q 9 8 3
              ♣ 2
♠ 8 7 4 3                      ♠ 9 6 5
♡ 10 8 4          N            ♡ Q 9 3 2
◇ 10          W       E        ◇ K J 4
♣ A Q 8 5 3       S            ♣ K 7 6
              ♠ Q 10
              ♡ A J 6
              ◇ 7 6 5 2
              ♣ J 10 9 4
```

You have eight top tricks – four spades, two hearts, one diamond and the club you have just made. Both of the red suits offer good prospects for contributing the extra trick you need. In each case, the best play if you consider one suit in isolation is to take a finesse (perhaps after cashing the ♡K in case of a bare ♡Q). Indeed, if you were playing match-point pairs, you might well view the situation that way.

Playing teams with IMP scoring (or rubber bridge), making the contract is the main goal and you often accept the risk of an extra undertrick if, by doing so, you increase the chance of making the contract. (You may have noticed that on the previous board you risked going about four down to give yourself the best chance of bringing home the slam.)

This approach means you should look to combine your chances in the red suits. Maybe the most natural way to do so is to cash the ace and king of hearts and, if the queen does not fall, fall back on the diamond finesse. However, other things being equal, trying to drop a bare ◇K with the heart finesse in reserve offers more or less the same odds of success (and may entail going rather less down if both chances fail).

From the play to the first two tricks it surely looks like West began with five clubs to East's three. This makes taking a finesse against East more attractive as Sally's hand has more room left in it for the key red cards. Of course, one need not rely on this information alone. Before taking your decision, cash four rounds of spades. If West has three or more, you will read him for more black cards than his partner, and play for the heart finesse (or diamond drop). If West turns up with no more than two spades, you will go for the diamond finesse (or heart drop).

Win the Big Match

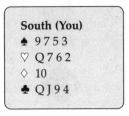

South (You)
♠ 9 7 5 3
♡ Q 7 6 2
♢ 10
♣ Q J 9 4

Sally on your right opens 1♢ and you pass, as does Wayne. Pat protects with 2♣ and Sally doubles. You have few values, fewer even than partner probably hoped for, but four-card support is a bonus. You could show decent values and club support with 2♢, so on your actual hand you can afford to bid 3♣. Wayne next bids 3♢ and Pat competes to 4♣. After this, Sally surprisingly introduces a new suit: 4♠. Nobody has any more to say and 4♠ becomes the final contract.

West	North	East	South
Wayne	*Pat*	*Sally*	*You*
		1♢	Pass
Pass	2♣	Dbl	3♣
3♢	4♣	4♠	All Pass

You lead the ♣Q and this holds the first trick.

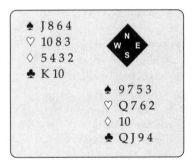

♠ J 8 6 4
♡ 10 8 3
♢ 5 4 3 2
♣ K 10

♠ 9 7 5 3
♡ Q 7 6 2
♢ 10
♣ Q J 9 4

You continue clubs and declarer, after pushing her hair back behind her ears, flamboyantly ruffs with the ♠A. She continues by cashing the ♠K, all following and then plays the ♠10 to the jack, partner discarding a middle club. Having now got to dummy, declarer leads a diamond to the jack and queen and then lays down the ace. How should you proceed?

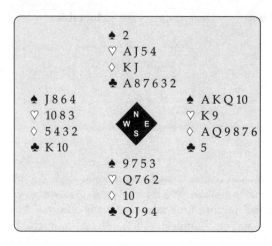

You know the precise layout of the black suits and you have a fair idea of the situation in diamonds as well. It looks like declarer's play of a diamond to the queen was a finesse against the king and it would seem that the king is about to fall. After all, why would Pat play the jack from K-J-x?

You could ruff, of course, but will this defeat the contract? You could persevere with clubs but, as you are down to one trump, declarer can afford to ruff in dummy; if she has the ♡K, she even has a choice of what to throw from hand. Trying a heart after ruffing at least gives you a chance, but it seems a very slim one since the ace-king of hearts would make Pat rather strong for a protective overall.

Suppose, then, that you discard. Well, if you keep allowing diamonds to win, the contract will make. Six diamonds, a ruff and three trump tricks add up to ten. So, sooner or later, you will need to ruff. How can you arrange to be in a position to do something deadly when eventually you do? Although you have four hearts, the answer is to play for a heart ruff! Start by discarding three hearts on the diamonds.

Having come down to one heart, you ruff the fifth round of diamonds high. You then play a heart to Pat's hoped-for ace and score a ruff. 'Gee, you guys defend well,' Wayne, who has been following the play closely, will say if you beat the game.

BOARD 23   Dealer: South. Game All.

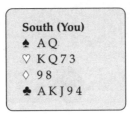

South (You)
♠ A Q
♡ K Q 7 3
◇ 9 8
♣ A K J 9 4

You have a useful collection, but not enough to open other than at the one level. If the bidding goes 1♣, all pass, you rarely figure to have missed game. To open 2NT with a 2-4-2-5 can work on occasion but you do not have good intermediates or such other feature as to justify upgrading your hand. Wayne passes, Pat responds 1◇ and Sally overcalls 3♠. Opposing pre-empts can force you to guess and this one seems to have succeeded. 4♡ could be the right contract if you find four hearts opposite, but Pat may give preference to 5♣ and put you uncomfortably high. With two spade stoppers, 3NT seems the practical shot. Wayne raises to 4♠ and, when this comes back, you double.

West	North	East	South
Wayne	*Pat*	*Sally*	*You*
			1♣
Pass	1◇	3♠	3NT
4♠	Pass	Pass	Dbl
All Pass			

You lead the ♣A and dummy differs from what you hoped for.

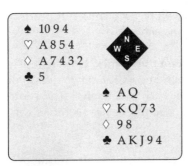

♠ 10 9 4
♡ A 8 5 4
◇ A 7 4 3 2
♣ 5

♠ A Q
♡ K Q 7 3
◇ 9 8
♣ A K J 9 4

Pat follows with the ♣2, which looks like a suit-preference signal as you both know no more clubs are cashing. How should you continue?

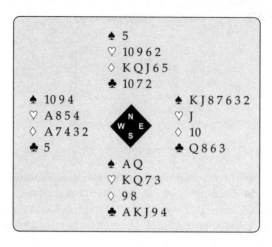

```
                    ♠ 5
                    ♡ 10 9 6 2
                    ◊ K Q J 6 5
                    ♣ 10 7 2
     ♠ 10 9 4                      ♠ K J 8 7 6 3 2
     ♡ A 8 5 4         N           ♡ J
     ◊ A 7 4 3 2    W     E        ◊ 10
     ♣ 5              S            ♣ Q 8 6 3
                    ♠ A Q
                    ♡ K Q 7 3
                    ◊ 9 8
                    ♣ A K J 9 4
```

Pat has bid diamonds and appears to be showing strength in the suit and it may seem natural to try a diamond next. Just about the only time this could cost directly would be if declarer had ◊Q-x and two small hearts. Of course, the bidding precludes such a distribution. With only three hearts, four diamonds and, presumably, a singleton spade, Pat would possess five-card club support, which you would no doubt have heard about. Does this make a diamond switch correct?

If declarer has a 7-2-1-3 shape, you will defeat the contract with the passive diamond switch. Declarer can ruff two clubs in dummy but will have to lose two trump tricks and a heart. Similarly, if she is 7-1-2-3, she will presumably have to lose two trumps and a diamond.

Unfortunately, defending passively will not work if declarer turns up with a 7-1-1-4 or a 7-2-0-4 shape. Dummy's aces will take care of her two red cards and Sally will happily cross-ruff hearts and clubs, just losing two trump tricks at the end.

It gives up your second trump trick, but might playing ace and another trump sometimes gain? You will stop two ruffs in dummy, so indeed the investment may come back with interest. This strategy certainly works a treat as the cards lie. Declarer makes six trump tricks, two aces but only one ruff.

Does any danger attach to this assault on trumps? Well, if declarer has ♡J-10 in a 7-2-1-3 shape, you allow an otherwise failing contract to make. This risk also applies if she has ♡J-10-x (or maybe J-9-x), but this sounds even less likely, as that would leave Pat with ten cards in the minors – surely not a hand for choosing to defend 4♠ doubled.

Dealer: West. Love All.

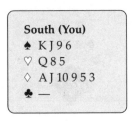

South (You)
♠ K J 9 6
♡ Q 8 5
♢ A J 10 9 5 3
♣ —

Fourth in hand, you watch as Wayne opens 1♣ and Sally responds 1♠. After you overcall 2♢, Wayne passes and Sally produces an alert card, which tells you that a special significance attaches to his pass. They play a convention known as 'support doubles', by which a double from opener would show three-card spade support, a raise four-card support and any other action (passing included) denies spade support. Sally reopens with 4♢, a splinter bid, showing big club support and at most one diamond. Wayne cue bids 4♡ and Sally cue bids 4♠. On the auction to date, a spade lead sounds like it would be welcome and you double this. Wayne tries to sign off in 5♣ but Sally calls the slam.

West	North	East	South
Wayne	*Pat*	*Sally*	*You*
1♣	Pass	1♠	2♢
Pass	Pass	4♢	Pass
4♡	Pass	4♠	Double
5♣	Pass	6♣	All Pass

Pat obediently leads the ♠5 and this is what you can see:

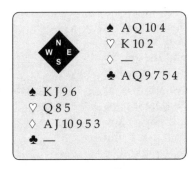

♠ A Q 10 4
♡ K 10 2
♢ —
♣ A Q 9 7 5 4

♠ K J 9 6
♡ Q 8 5
♢ A J 10 9 5 3
♣ —

Declarer smiles at Sally 'Very pretty!' and calls for the queen from dummy. You win with king. Can you find a safe return?

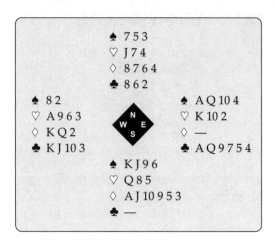

♠ 7 5 3
♡ J 7 4
◇ 8 7 6 4
♣ 8 6 2

♠ 8 2
♡ A 9 6 3
◇ K Q 2
♣ K J 10 3

♠ A Q 10 4
♡ K 10 2
◇ —
♣ A Q 9 7 5 4

♠ K J 9 6
♡ Q 8 5
◇ A J 10 9 5 3
♣ —

If you had a trump, you probably would have returned one by now, but fate has denied you this option. Waiting a long time in the hope that one of the other players thinks they have the lead will not work in a Gold Cup final, so you will need to lead something.

Dummy's tenace makes the risk with a spade return clear. If declarer has three hearts and two spades, the extra winner will enable him to get rid of any third-round heart loser. A diamond switch also looks highly dangerous. One struggles to see how Wayne has an opening bid, let alone enough to co-operate in the slam hunt, without the ◇K. This means that whether you lead a high or low diamond, you will allow the king to score and dummy's third heart to disappear. This leaves hearts. You might get away with a quick ♡Q (if Wayne plays you for the ♡J), but it is too late for that! If Pat has ♡J-9-x you can lead a low heart without blowing a trick immediately, but you set yourself up for a squeeze.

Wayne can ruff two spades in hand and at the end you will be unable to keep two hearts and the ◇A. To succeed, you must accept defeat if Wayne has only three hearts and focus on stopping the slam if he is 2-4-3-4 or 2-4-2-5 with no ♡J. You do this by returning a spade into the jaws of dummy's tenace. One heart discard from hand does him no good and you can defend the ending (right) by letting one heart go at some stage.

♠ —
♡ J 7 4
◇ 8 7
♣ —

♠ —
♡ A 9 6
◇ K Q
♣ —

♠ A
♡ K 10 2
◇ —
♣ 7

♠ —
♡ Q 8 5
◇ A J
♣ —

RESULTS ON BOARDS 17-24

Looking fairly contented, Chris and Alex arrive. 'We've nothing to be ashamed off,' Alex remarks, before asking if you can say the same.

A system difference affected the result on Board 17. Chris and Alex play Michaels cue bids, but restrict them to weak and strong hands. They exclude the intermediate range to avoid having to guess whether to bid on after a minimum response from partner. So, when Suzanne played in 4♠ after Alex had overcalled 2♡, she had less warning of the bad breaks and, ruffing the third heart, went one down. This means you win 10 IMPs if you made 4♠; otherwise, the board is flat.

On Board 18, when you needed an avoidance play to extract Sally's exit cards, the auction took a different course in the other room. Non-vulnerable, Chris and Alex play a weak 1NT. Chris duly opened 1NT and Suzanne doubled. Alex ran to 2◊ and Lucy doubled, which on their methods is for take-out. Suzanne, with ◊A-K-Q-x, left the double in. They defended well and collected 500.

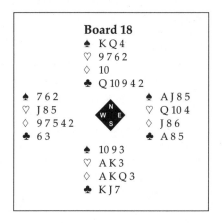

Board 18

♠ K Q 4
♡ 9 7 6 2
◊ 10
♣ Q 10 9 4 2

♠ 7 6 2   ♠ A J 8 5
♡ J 8 5   ♡ Q 10 4
◊ 9 7 5 4 2   ◊ J 8 6
♣ 6 3   ♣ A 8 5

♠ 10 9 3
♡ A K 3
◊ A K Q 3
♣ K J 7

This means you win 4 IMPs if you made 3NT with an overtrick (the way East defended) or lose 12 if you went off.

On Board 19, Lucy found the lead to kill 4♠. As at your table, South had bid diamonds twice, but Lucy led a club, finding her partner with A-Q-x over K-J. So, the board is flat if you beat 4♠; letting it make would cost 12 IMPs.

North (Lucy)

♠ 8 6 4
♡ K 7 3
◊ 10 4
♣ 10 8 5 3 2

Lucy did not bid 3♡ over the 3◊ pre-empt with a 3-6-2-2 10-count on Board 20, as Pat did. They were never going to reach a slam now and Suzanne made twelve tricks in 3NT on the ◊8 lead. So, you gain 13 IMPs if you made 6NT or lose this amount if you went one or two down.

Like you, they reached 3NT on Board 21, but Suzanne missed the best line. After getting in with the club and running the spades, she cashed the top hearts (East had thrown one) and, when the queen did not drop, tried the diamond finesse. This means you gain 13 IMPs if you made 3NT or 3 IMPs if you went one off; two off gives a flat board.

Perhaps not foreseeing the communication difficulties declarer would have in 4♠ on Board 22 (the deal on which your opponents had a fit in spades and diamonds), Lucy and Suzanne in the other room chose to sacrifice in 5♣ doubled. This gave your team +300 and offers you the chance to win 9 IMPs by beating 4♠. If you let it through, you lose 8.

Wayne and Sally did quite well to bid 4♠ over 3NT on Board 23 when vulnerable, and you are not surprised to find that Chris and Alex defended 3NT. Alex led the ♠10, which knocked out the first of declarer's spade stoppers, but as the cards lay, Suzanne could hardly go down. In practice, she took the ♣A, sneaked through a diamond and ran the ♣10. After repeating the finesse, she drove out the ♡A to end with eleven tricks.

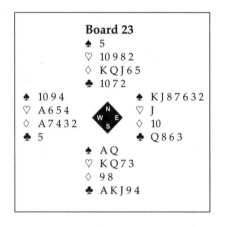

Board 23

♠ 5
♡ 10 9 8 2
◊ K Q J 6 5
♣ 10 7 2

♠ 10 9 4   ♠ K J 8 7 6 3 2
♡ A 6 5 4   ♡ J
◊ A 7 4 3 2   ◊ 10
♣ 5   ♣ Q 8 6 3

♠ A Q
♡ K Q 7 3
◊ 9 8
♣ A K J 9 4

The unfortunate effect of this result is that holding your loss to 10 IMPs by beating 4♠ doubled constitutes the best you can do. If you allowed it to make, I am afraid you lose a double-game swing and 16 IMPs.

On Board 24, not for first time, a systemic difference affected events. Using, as you know, a weak no-trump non-vulnerable, Alex opened 1NT and, on the 4-3-0-6 hand you saw in dummy, Chris responded 2♣, Stayman. This meant that when Chris and Alex also reached 6♣, Suzanne, with your 4-3-6-0 11-count, was on lead, making their slam unbeatable. If you found the correct return to defeat 6♣, you therefore pick up 14 IMPs. If you missed it, you escape with a flat board.

Having played three sets without a break, you will not mind if Chris decides to give you a rest now, but this is not to be. The opponents have the choice of line-up on the fourth set and you will return to doing battle with Lucy and Suzanne in the open room. At the other table, Sam and Phil will come back in to play against Wayne and Sally.

BOARD 25   Dealer: North. E/W Vulnerable.

> **South (You)**
> ♠ Q942
> ♡ A3
> ◇ 94
> ♣ J9653

Pat passes as dealer, Suzanne on your right opens 1♡ and you pass. Lucy also passes and Pat reopens with a double. Suzanne redoubles and three options present themselves: (1) you could pass; this is not now a penalty pass, (2) you could bid your four-card major or (3) you could call 2♣. Passing is unlikely to help; at best, you defer a decision to the next round. The real choice lies between 1♠ and 2♣, and the likelihood that someone will compete to 2♡ determines the best action. If you bid 1♠ now and 2♠ later, you may find yourself in a 4-3 spade fit instead of a 5-4 club fit. Equally, if you bid 1♠ and then 3♣ and Pat has four spades, you get to 3♠ instead of 2♠. The prepared action is to start with 2♣, and the auction unfolds as follows:

West	North	East	South
Lucy	Pat	Suzanne	You
	Pass	1♡	Pass
Pass	Dbl	Redbl	2♣
2♡	Pass	Pass	2♠
Pass	3♣	3♡	All Pass

You lead the ◇9 and partner's king wins.

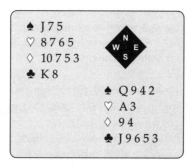

> ♠ J75
> ♡ 8765
> ◇ 10753
> ♣ K8
>
> ♠ Q942
> ♡ A3
> ◇ 94
> ♣ J9653

Pat cashes the ◇A at trick two and continues with the ◇2. Declarer, who has followed low twice, now plays the queen. What is your plan?

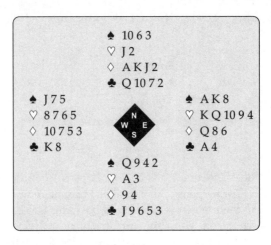

♠ 10 6 3
♡ J 2
♢ A K J 2
♣ Q 10 7 2

♠ J 7 5
♡ 8 7 6 5
♢ 10 7 5 3
♣ K 8

♠ A K 8
♡ K Q 10 9 4
♢ Q 8 6
♣ A 4

♠ Q 9 4 2
♡ A 3
♢ 9 4
♣ J 9 6 5 3

The bidding has given you a very good idea of the lie of the cards and no possible excuse exists for misdefending on this deal. Clearly, the spades are 4-3-3-3 round the table, or Pat would not have gone back to 3♣. Equally, the clubs must be 5-2-4-2, as with five-card support Pat would bid 3♣ directly over 2♡. This puts declarer's shape as 3-5-3-2.

You cannot be quite so sure of the high cards. Pat, having passed as dealer, can hold at most 11 points, eight of which you know (♢A-K-J). If declarer is missing one of the major-suit kings (just possible) then you can defeat the contract easily enough after ruffing the third round of diamonds. Can you still succeed if she has both?

With the ♠J on view in dummy, clearly you do not intend to lead a spade next, so suppose you exit passively with a club. All will turn out well if declarer simply plays on trumps, as you can play a second club. The snag is that Suzanne knows it can cost nothing to cash a second round of clubs herself. Then, having got in with the ♡A, you will face the unattractive choice of broaching the spades or conceding a ruff and discard. To avoid this scenario, cash the ♡A at trick four before exiting with a club. This way your spade trick cannot run away.

Part-score deals generate less excitement than games and slams, and produce smaller swings. Even so, they can play an important part in a long match. If you lose 110 instead of making it or, as could happen on this deal, concede 140 when you should be collecting 50 or 100, you may lose 6 or 5 IMPs. Two modest swings like this come to as much as a game swing. You will therefore find that people contest part-score deals almost as fiercely as they would at match-point pairs.

BOARD 26   Dealer: East. Game All.

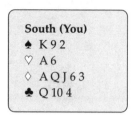

South (You)
♠ K 9 2
♡ A 6
◇ A Q J 6 3
♣ Q 10 4

Suzanne, as East, opens 1♠ and this time you have only two choices: 2◇ and 1NT. Both have their advantages and disadvantages. Bidding 2◇ may help you to compete if it is part-score deal and partner has diamond support. It could also work well if you belong in no-trumps but the contract plays better from partner's hand, say if Pat has ♠Q-x. 1NT, however, describes the strength and nature of your hand better and may help you in reaching game and getting to the right one. You decide to call 1NT and, after a Stayman enquiry, find yourself in 3NT.

West	North	East	South
Lucy	*Pat*	*Suzanne*	*You*
		1♠	1NT
Pass	2♣	Pass	2◇
Pass	3NT	All Pass	

West leads the ♠5, and you are glad to see Pat does not have ♠Q-x.

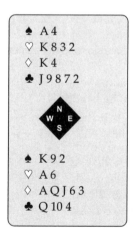

♠ A 4
♡ K 8 3 2
◇ K 4
♣ J 9 8 7 2

♠ K 9 2
♡ A 6
◇ A Q J 6 3
♣ Q 10 4

How do you play for nine tricks?

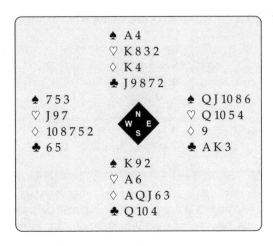

If the diamonds break no worse than 4-2 then you have nine top tricks: five diamonds and two ace-kings. What can you do about a 5-1 split?

If the ace and king of clubs lie in opposite hands and the lead is a singleton then you can win the first trick and set up the clubs. Also, in case the top clubs are split and spades are 6-2, you could duck the first trick. A heart switch might cause a problem on some layouts but, on a spade continuation, you will have time to enjoy the clubs. Of course, it seems unlikely that West holds ♠5-3 alone or a bare ♠5. In any case, for her vulnerable opening, you expect East to hold the top clubs.

With diamonds 5-1 and both club entries with East, do you have any chance? The answer is yes, and it appears quite a reasonable one if West is the one with five diamonds. You simply need East to hold four (or five) hearts. Then you should be able to squeeze her in three suits.

To maintain communications, you must win the first trick in hand with the king. You can then play three (or four) rounds of diamonds, throwing one club (or two) from dummy. Suzanne parts with one club, but soon feels the pressure. If she lets go a spade, you can afford to play on clubs, losing two clubs and just two spades. A second club discard is obviously fatal and, if she discards a heart, you play three rounds of the suit, getting to the long card with the ♠A.

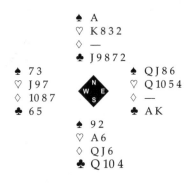

she discards a heart, you play three rounds of the suit, getting to the long card with the ♠A.

> **South (You)**
> ♠ J 8
> ♡ A 9 8 5 3
> ◇ K J 7
> ♣ A Q 8

As dealer, you could downgrade the hand to a weak no-trump, which is what you play non-vulnerable, but there seems no particular reason to do so. After you open 1♡, Lucy overcalls 2♣. This is weak, though not suicidally so at equal vulnerability. Pat jumps to 4♡, which is also weak(!); with a decent hand, Pat would cue-bid 3♣. Suzanne bids 4♠ and it is you to bid again. You have a bit more strength than your opening showed, with just a single point wasted in spades. However, given your balanced shape, this would not justify going to 5♡. Perhaps a double tickles your fancy. After all, you could score three defensive tricks, possibly more if the cards lie well for your side. If you do act, double is better than 5♡, but your hand really has nothing sufficiently special about it to warrant taking any action. Your pass is not forcing as Pat's raise was weak and indeed 4♠ becomes the final contract.

West	North	East	South
Lucy	*Pat*	*Suzanne*	*You*
			1♡
2♣	4♡	4♠	All Pass

Pat leads the ♣J and you have mixed feelings about the dummy.

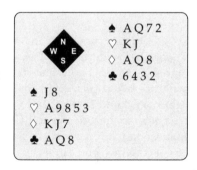

                    ♠ A Q 7 2
                    ♡ K J
                    ◇ A Q 8
                    ♣ 6 4 3 2
    ♠ J 8
    ♡ A 9 8 5 3
    ◇ K J 7
    ♣ A Q 8

Clearly, 5♡ would fail. Can you defeat 4♠?

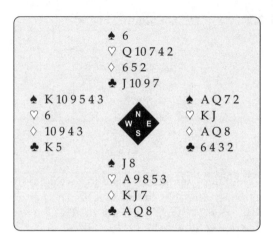

If declarer has a heart, you can count one trick in the suit. Assuming she has the ♣K, you can count on one club as well. The diamond layout looks helpful, since you have the king-jack over the ace-queen and the potential to score two tricks. Can you afford to sit back?

Suppose you go up with the ♣A and return the queen. Declarer will win, go to dummy with a trump, ruff a club, go back over with a trump and ruff another club. Now she may play a heart to the jack, though you would still be in trouble if the king went up. You return a heart and declarer can ruff even if dummy has the winner, and lead a diamond. All will be well if partner has the ◊10-9. If not, Pat's card is covered to leave you endplayed.

To avoid getting into this situation, you need to arrange for a diamond lead through the ace-queen before declarer has removed your exit cards. In three out of the four suits, there is no chance of creating an entry in partner's hand. Playing the ♣Q at trick one is the only way to do so. After this start, Suzanne can do no better than to draw two rounds of trumps before leading a heart to the jack and ace. Then you exit with the ♣8 and Pat should manage to work out what to do. It is just too bad if declarer is 6-1-3-3 or 6-0-4-3, as then you cannot expect to set the contract even if partner has ◊10-9-x(-x). Nor, unless Pat has ◊10-9 bare, could you ever hope for success against a 6-1-5-1 shape.

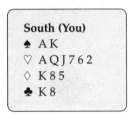

South (You)
♠ A K
♡ A Q J 7 6 2
◇ K 8 5
♣ K 8

Lucy opens 1NT and, after a pass from partner, Suzanne bids 2♡, a transfer. As the opening was weak, you double to show a good hand (the heart holding is coincidental). Lucy completes the transfer with 2♠, promising, on their methods, at least three-card spade support. Pat passes and Suzanne raises to 3♠! Decision time has come. Do you reckon two stoppers will give you time for nine tricks in no-trumps? If not, can Pat produce the fillers for you to lose only three tricks in 4♡ as trumps? It seems a guess, and you try 4♡, which buys the contract.

West	North	East	South
Lucy	*Pat*	*Suzanne*	*You*
1NT	Pass	2♡	Dbl
2♠	Pass	3♠	4♡
All Pass			

West studies the bidding and her cards carefully before leading the ♡10 and you are glad to see 3NT has only eight tricks.

♠ Q 10
♡ K 5 4 3
◇ J 7
♣ 9 7 6 4 2

♠ A K
♡ A Q J 7 6 2
◇ K 8 5
♣ K 8

That is very well, but can you make ten tricks with hearts as trumps?

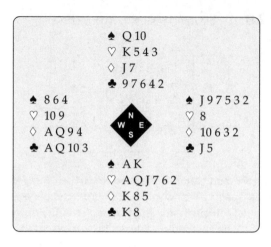

On a different auction, you might simply use the ♡K as an entry for trying a diamond to the king. Then, if that lost, a diamond ruff would put you back in dummy for testing your luck in clubs. Here, with just 14 points missing, you know Lucy holds both minor-suit aces.

Prospects for setting up any long clubs do not look good. Aside from the danger that East may get in, entries to dummy present a problem. A throw-in seems the order of the day. How should you set about it?

It looks natural to win the first trick in hand, unblock the spades and draw trumps ending in dummy, leading the ♡6 to the king. Now you stand a good chance of being able to put Lucy on play by running the ◊J. What good, though, does it do? She simply wins with the queen, cashes the ace and exits with a third round to leave you with two inescapable club losers. Instead your exit has to take place in clubs.

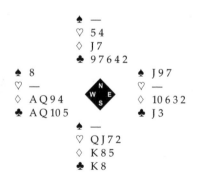

If East plays low on the club, you must restrain yourself from going up with the king. West might win with the ace and get off play with a low club. Instead, play the ♣8. West wins and a diamond or spade lead now will solve all your problems. Cashing the ♣A provides her with a temporary escape but, with the ♣J falling, she is then really stuck. Whether she leads a low or high club, one ruff sets up the suit, giving you two diamond discards.

Win the Big Match

BOARD 29   Dealer: North. Game All.

> **South (You)**
> ♠ K 8 7 2
> ♡ A 6 4 3
> ◇ A Q 9 3
> ♣ K

Pat, North, opens 1♣ and East, passes. Modern bidding tends to put emphasis on the majors, but one must take care not to carry a good idea to extremes. Imagine facing ♣A-Q-J-x-x-x and four diamonds to the king or king-jack. Then you would want to play in 6◇, yet partner may have too little to reverse; besides you would prefer to be declarer to protect the ♠K. You, therefore, respond 1◇ and Pat rebids 2♣. Opposite a minimum opening, and knowing that no fit exists, you should give up any thoughts of a slam if partner holds perfect cards and make the pragmatic bid of what you think you can make: 3NT.

West	North	East	South
Lucy	*Pat*	*Suzanne*	*You*
	1♣	Pass	1◇
Pass	2♣	Pass	3NT
All Pass			

West leads the ♡2 and Pat puts down just about what you expected: a six-card club suit and minimum values. How you do plan the play?

> ♠ A 4 3
> ♡ K 8 5
> ◇ 6
> ♣ A 10 9 8 7 3
>
>   N
> W   E
>   S
>
> ♠ K 8 7 2
> ♡ A 6 4 3
> ◇ A Q 9 3
> ♣ K

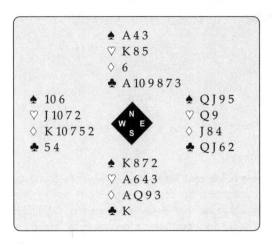

```
                    ♠ A 4 3
                    ♡ K 8 5
                    ◊ 6
                    ♣ A 10 9 8 7 3
    ♠ 10 6                            ♠ Q J 9 5
    ♡ J 10 7 2          N            ♡ Q 9
    ◊ K 10 7 5 2    W       E        ◊ J 8 4
    ♣ 5 4              S             ♣ Q J 6 2
                    ♠ K 8 7 2
                    ♡ A 6 4 3
                    ◊ A Q 9 3
                    ♣ K
```

If the cards lie well, you could make eleven tricks: five clubs and two in each of the other suits. Playing teams, however, making the contract must be your primary objective, so you look to see how to overcome possible bad breaks.

Suppose you win the opening lead in hand (entries to dummy appear scarce), unblock the ♣K and cross to the ♠A. You continue with ace and another club. All will be well if clubs break 3-3 or the defender short in clubs has the queen or jack, as in that case you can obviously set up the clubs for one loser. As the cards lie, you have a problem. The clubs are not good and you have only one entry left to dummy. Unable to use the clubs, it seems most unlikely that you can come to nine tricks. In essence, you would need the diamond finesse to work and spades to break 3-3. On the actual layout, you will need to throw West in to lead from the ◊K to get out for one down.

Four club tricks will suffice for your contract and you should play for these by overtaking the ♣K with the ace. The defenders surely have two club stoppers now, but you can afford to lose two hearts and two clubs. (The opening lead marks the hearts as no worse than 4-2.)

Ah, but suppose the defenders do not continue hearts and switch to diamonds instead. Then the 100% safe line is to play the ace on the first round and cover East's card on the second round. This way you will lose two clubs, no hearts and at most two diamonds. Today, the lie of the cards will forgive a sub-optimal strategy, as you can play any diamond on the first round and survive. You just need to get the clubs right to score nine tricks.

BOARD 30   Dealer: East. Love All.

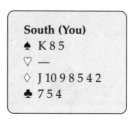

South (You)
♠ K 8 5
♡ —
◇ J 10 9 8 5 4 2
♣ 7 5 4

Suzanne, East, opens 1♣, and it is your bid now. You play weak jump overcalls, but normally these show only six cards at the two-level. Yes, the suit is poor, but the void more than makes up for this. You stand a far better chance of disrupting the opponents' auction if you take out two rounds of bidding. On average partner will have two diamonds to go with your seven, giving you a nine-card fit; this means, according to the 'Law of Total Tricks', that it should be safe to go to the three level. A little to your surprise, Pat raises to 5◇, and this ends the bidding:

West	North	East	South
Lucy	*Pat*	*Suzanne*	*You*
		1♣	3◇
Pass	5◇	All Pass	

West leads the ◇6 and you soon see why nobody doubled.

♠ A Q 10 2
♡ Q 10 4 2
◇ A K Q
♣ 8 3

♠ K 8 5
♡ —
◇ J 10 9 8 5 4 2
♣ 7 5 4

You must win in dummy and East discards the ♣Q as if it were a bag of the pumpkin seeds she keeps chewing. What is your plan?

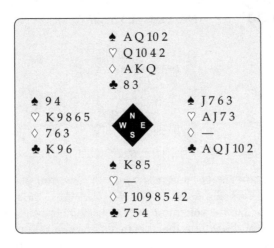

The 3-0 trump break, coupled with the initial assault on the suit, makes life complicated. Now you cannot be sure of being able to ruff a club in dummy. The spade suit offers another possible source of an eleventh trick, if spades break 3-3 or the jack falls in two rounds. A further idea is to ruff three hearts in hand in the hope that East has A-K-x; then the ♡Q would become good. Actually, in some circumstances, it might help to ruff four rounds of hearts, since you might obtain a sufficiently good idea of the distribution to get to know to finesse West for the ♠J.

Despite what has happened at trick one, you still have a reasonable chance of obtaining a club ruff in dummy. If Lucy has K-6-2, K-6 or K-2, she cannot get in twice. You also appear well placed if Lucy has K-9 (or K-10) doubleton. If her shape is 3-5-3-2, the spades will produce four tricks; if it is 2-6-3-2, you may well have a squeeze against East. If you take care, you can also cope with the likes of K-9-6 in Lucy's hand.

The trick is to ruff a heart at trick two and lead a low club. Lucy must go in with ♣9 to continue trumps. After dummy wins, you can ruff a heart and lead another club. Now she must play the king to lead a third round of trumps; again you win in dummy and can ruff a heart. Now, when you lead your last trump and the ♡K does not appear, dummy throws the ♡Q. With your

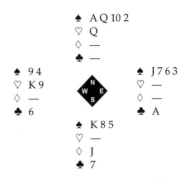

♣7 a threat against her, East is squeezed in the black suits.

BOARD 31 — Dealer: South. N/S Vulnerable.

> **South (You)**
> ♠ J 4
> ♡ 10 7 6 2
> ◇ A K Q J 10 6
> ♣ A

First in hand, you open 1◇. With the opponents silent, Pat responds 1♠ and you must find a rebid. Terence Reese said: 'Don't bid a bad suit on a good hand', and his advice still holds true. A reverse to 2♡ would misdescribe this hand, so you jump to 3◇. Over this, Pat rebids 3♠ and you are close to making an advance cue-bid of 4♣. However, you settle for 4♠. Pat cue bids 5♡ and, holding first-round control in the unbid suit, you should co-operate. Intending to offer a choice of slams, you try 6◇. Pat seems to take it this way, as 6◇ becomes the final contract.

West	North	East	South
Lucy	*Pat*	*Suzanne*	*You*
			1◇
Pass	1♠	Pass	3◇
Pass	3♠	Pass	4♠
Pass	5♡	Pass	6◇
All Pass			

Having rolled her pen a couple of times, West leads the ♣J and the slam looks good. What is the best line?

> ♠ A K 7 5 3 2
> ♡ A Q 4
> ◇ 7 3
> ♣ Q 7
>
> ♠ J 4
> ♡ 10 7 6 2
> ◇ A K Q J 10 6
> ♣ A

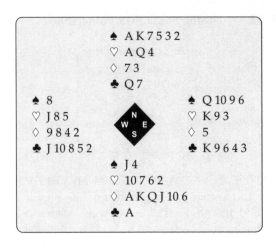

```
              ♠ A K 7 5 3 2
              ♡ A Q 4
              ◇ 7 3
              ♣ Q 7
  ♠ 8                        ♠ Q 10 9 6
  ♡ J 8 5        N           ♡ K 9 3
  ◇ 9 8 4 2    W   E         ◇ 5
  ♣ J 10 8 5 2   S           ♣ K 9 6 4 3
              ♠ J 4
              ♡ 10 7 6 2
              ◇ A K Q J 10 6
              ♣ A
```

You have ten top tricks – six trumps, two spades and two aces. Both major suits offer scope for making up the difference. Indeed, having escaped (if that is the right word) a heart lead, you can make all the tricks if spades break 3-2.

One line is to win the club, draw trumps and then play ace, king and ruff a spade. If the spades split 3-2, you can probably claim the rest of the tricks (it depends upon what you have thrown from dummy). If not, you continue by taking the heart finesse. If this succeeds, again you emerge with an overtrick. Unfortunately, if somebody shows out on the second round of spades and East turns up with the ♡K, you appear almost out of options. Even if the ♡J is due to fall doubleton, a heart return will sever the link to dummy and leave you with very few chances. Most likely, you would be reduced to hoping that West has ♡J-9 or ♡J-8 bare, in which case you could finesse the seven on the third round of hearts.

Clearly, it would not help you to play on hearts before spades. If East turns up with the ♡K and West the ♡J, you might go down even with spades 3-2. The solution is to lose the first round of spades. Then, even on a 4-1 split, a single ruff will set up the suit. Naturally, you must exercise care in *how* you duck a spade. You do not want West to win and lead a heart through dummy's ace-queen. Having drawn trumps, you must follow Rixi Markus's 'If you are going to duck, duck high' rule and lead the ♠J, intending to run it. If West covers, you will have to win in dummy and hope that one of the major suits behaves reasonably kindly. In practice, West cannot beat the ♠J; East, after scoring the ♠Q, cannot attack dummy's heart entry, so the slam makes.

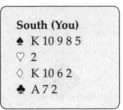

South (You)
♠ K 10 9 8 5
♡ 2
◇ K 10 6 2
♣ A 7 2

Lucy opens 2♠, which shows 6-10 points and a six-card spade suit. Pat doubles, for take-out, and Suzanne passes.

Ordinarily, you remove take-out doubles, especially when the contract, if it makes, would give the opponents game. That sort of result can turn out just as expensive as it would at rubber bridge. Sitting under the bidder, you need good trumps to contemplate defending. Here you appear to have them, and you hold sufficient values to expect that your side possesses the balance of power. This second factor could prove as decisive as the first. The fewer high cards dummy has, the lesser the risk that declarer can win lots of trump tricks by taking finesses against you or by ruffs in the long hand. With this collection, you would probably pass even if the opponents were non-vulnerable (since you cannot be sure of game), and are delighted to do so when they are.

West	North	East	South
Lucy	Pat	Suzanne	You
2♠	Dbl	All Pass	

Pat leads the ♣10 and you capture dummy's jack with the ace.

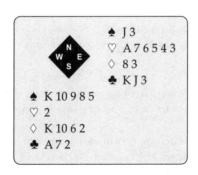

♠ J 3
♡ A 7 6 5 4 3
◇ 8 3
♣ K J 3

♠ K 10 9 8 5
♡ 2
◇ K 10 6 2
♣ A 7 2

What should you return for the maximum penalty?

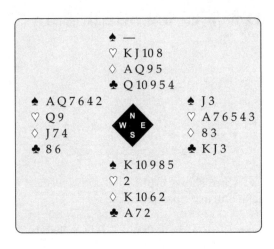

You can almost write down the 52-card diagram from the bidding and play to trick one. Declarer must have the six trumps you cannot see and, as Pat might have led a heart from K-Q-J or K-Q-10 in preference to a club from Q-10-9, you place Lucy with the ♡Q. She should not have any more significant high cards because (a) with them she would have opened 1♠, and (b) Pat's double would then be very thin.

Dummy's doubleton in diamonds poses the threat and, to prevent declarer from scoring a ruff or a cheap trick with the ♠7, it may look natural to return the ♠10. Now watch what happens if you do. Declarer wins in dummy and, say, plays a diamond. You win and play the ♠9, which loses to the queen. Lucy can now play a club to the king and ruff a club, then cash the

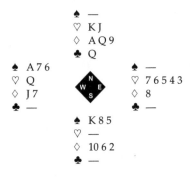

♡A and wait for two more trump tricks – one down.

Even if declarer's shape were 6-2-2-3, she would still avoid going two down after your ♠10 switch. She would win it in dummy, play a round of trumps, covering your card, and eventually score five trump tricks.

As the cards lie, switching to the ♠K does not work either and the solution is to lead the ♠5 at trick two. Declarer wins with the six, but her joy is short-lived. When you get in with a diamond, you will lead the ♠K, squashing dummy's jack. She can use the ♣K as an entry to ruff a club, but she lacks the transportation to score a second ruff.

RESULTS ON BOARDS 25-32

'We've conceded a few penalties', says Sam arriving, 'but we've more pluses'. 'Yes', Phil adds, 'apart from a game they missed, everything went down.' You respond with brief comments about your results.

On Board 25, the bidding at the other table began the same way, pass-1♡-pass-pass-double, but Phil rebid 1NT rather than redoubling. Sally did as you did, trying 2♣ as her first move and then 2♠ over West's 2♡, but the different tempo to the auction left her to play quietly in 3♣, going down one, giving 50 to East-West (2♠ would also be one off). This means you gain 4 IMPs if you beat 3♡ or lose 3 if you allowed it to make.

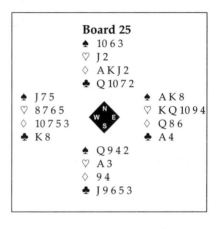

Board 25

♠ 10 6 3
♡ J 2
◇ A K J 2
♣ Q 10 7 2

♠ J 7 5   ♠ A K 8
♡ 8 7 6 5   ♡ K Q 10 9 4
◇ 10 7 5 3   ◇ Q 8 6
♣ K 8   ♣ A 4

♠ Q 9 4 2
♡ A 3
◇ 9 4
♣ J 9 6 5 3

On Board 26 South also played in 3NT but Sally failed to see the three-suit squeeze and thought her only way to overcome a bad diamond break was to try to disrupt the defensive communications by holding up at the first trick. This meant Phil as East came under less pressure; with dummy's ♠A entry to the hearts gone, a heart discard was safe. If you made 3NT, you gain 12 IMPs; the board is flat if you went down.

On Board 27, the bidding began the same way but, once Sally did not double 4♠, Wayne thought it must be on and broke discipline, sacrificing in 5♡ doubled. Declarer lost one trick in each suit, giving Sam and Phil 300. Therefore, you win 8 IMPs if you defeated 4♠ or lose 3 if it made.

North (Wayne)
♠ 6
♡ Q 10 7 4 2
◇ 6 5 2
♣ J 10 9 7

Board 28 was similar to 27, though with the boot on the other foot. Phil, with the 6-1-4-2 hand including two jacks, knew of three-card support opposite and, when Sam did not double 4♡, decided to sacrifice in 4♠ doubled. With spades 2-2 (A-K bare facing Q-10 you recall) and both minors sitting well (as they were wrong for you!), this went only one down. So you win 11 IMPs if you made 4♡ or lose 5 if you went down.

On Board 29, when you played in 3NT with a 4-4-4-1 16-count, the bidding and lead were the same at the other table. Sally misplayed the clubs, allowing the ♣K to win, but she did find the throw-in to avoid the two-trick defeat. This means you win 12 IMPs if you made 3NT or lose 3 if you went two down. The board is flat if you went one down.

On Board 30 Wayne and Sally only bid to 4◇, and Sam led a club. So you will never find out whether Sally would have set up her ♣7 as a threat to squeeze Phil in the black suits. Team-mates' score of -150 means you gain 6 IMPs if you made 5◇ or lose 5 if you went down.

On Board 31, you did well to reach 6◇ having agreed spades (and to avoid what would have been a killing spade lead). The opponents were not up to the task in the other room. They bid 1◇-1♠-3◇-3♠-4♠-4NT-5♡-6♠. In essence the small slam in spades depends on a 3-2 trump break, so stood no hope on the actual layout. Phil could even have afforded to start with a heart into the ace-queen!

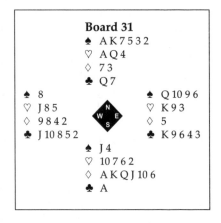

Board 31
♠ A K 7 5 3 2
♡ A Q 4
◇ 7 3
♣ Q 7

♠ 8
♡ J 8 5
◇ 9 8 4 2
♣ J 10 8 5 2

♠ Q 10 9 6
♡ K 9 3
◇ 5
♣ K 9 6 4 3

♠ J 4
♡ 10 7 6 2
◇ A K Q J 10 6
♣ A

This result means that you pick up a massive 16 IMPs if you made 6◇, and you still manage to tie the board if you went down.

The auction and play to the first trick on Board 32 were the same at the other table. Sally then switched to the ♠10, allowing Sam to get out for one down, losing 200. So, if you picked up 500 for two down, you gain 7 IMPs; the board is flat if you returned anything other than the ♠5.

Nobody can play 64 boards with only scoring breaks and you feel relieved when Pat reminds you that refreshment time has arrived. The match takes place in a hotel and the staff have laid on more food and drink than you could possibly consume. Playing bridge tends to take your mind off hunger, making it useful to have this interlude forced upon you. Needless to say, you must re-enter the fray having had your fill. In the open room, the line-up will be as in the first set, with you and Pat taking on Steve and Edgar. In the closed room, Alex and Chris will do battle with Lucy and Suzanne. I hope the wining and dining has not made you drowsy, as plenty of fresh challenges lie ahead. . .

BOARD 33   Dealer: North. Love All.

```
┌─────────────────────────┐
│   South (You)           │
│   ♠ A 5 4 2             │
│   ♡ —                   │
│   ◇ A K Q 10 8 4        │
│   ♣ J 8 2               │
└─────────────────────────┘
```

Third in hand, you open 1◇. Steve overcalls 1♡ and Pat doubles. This is a negative double, usually with four spades. Edgar raises to 2♡ and you have some choices. With a five-loser hand, a jump to 4♠ appears justified. If you disagree with that valuation, you could bid 3♠ instead. A cue-bid of 3♡ followed by 4♠ next time sounds wrong, suggesting more high cards than you have. What should an immediate 4♡ mean? You and Pat play a lot of splinter bids, and maybe this should be one. However, you cannot recall ever having discussed this auction, and the middle of a long match hardly seems a good time to spring something untried on partner. Playing safe, you settle for a simple 4♠.

West	North	East	South
Steve	*Pat*	*Edgar*	*You*
	Pass	Pass	1◇
1♡	Dbl	2♡	4♠
All Pass			

West strokes his chin a couple of times and leads the ♡K. How you do plan the play?

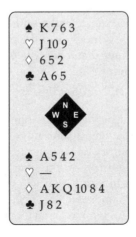

```
        ♠ K 7 6 3
        ♡ J 10 9
        ◇ 6 5 2
        ♣ A 6 5

           N
        W     E
           S

        ♠ A 5 4 2
        ♡ —
        ◇ A K Q 10 8 4
        ♣ J 8 2
```

```
                    ♠ K 7 6 3
                    ♡ J 10 9
                    ◇ 6 5 2
                    ♣ A 6 5
    ♠ J                           ♠ Q 10 9 8
    ♡ K Q 6 5 3 2    N            ♡ A 8 7 4
    ◇ 9 3          W   E          ◇ J 7
    ♣ K Q 4 3        S            ♣ 10 9 7
                    ♠ A 5 4 2
                    ♡ —
                    ◇ A K Q 10 8 4
                    ♣ J 8 2
```

Since the opening lead has not set up any defensive winners, you might make twelve tricks if trumps break 3-2. You just ruff, draw two rounds of trumps and turn to diamonds. At least you were right to think that the hand offers some potential for a slam facing a passed partner.

Suppose initially that you play as above. You ruff, play two rounds of trumps, and someone shows out. You will turn to diamonds, but even if three diamonds stand up, you will go down. Someone will ruff the fourth round and draw your last trump. Then you will be unable to get back to hand and dummy will be left with several losers.

Discarding a club at trick one can hardly help. A club switch will surely beat you if trumps break 4-1. Perhaps you do better to cash only one top trump (you must draw at least one round, or a defender with a singleton trump will eventually be able to ruff a diamond). This will reduce the danger that somebody can draw your trumps. Will cashing the ♠A work? It may do: you would need the defender with four trumps to hold three diamonds. In this case, he can only ruff the fourth round and you will score four trump tricks, three diamonds, the ♣A and two heart ruffs. Of course, such a layout is improbable; if Edgar or, more likely, Steve, has two singletons, he might well have competed to 5♡.

Nothing can be done if the defender with four trumps has one diamond, but you can cater for his having two (or more). You do this by using the ♠K to draw a round of trumps. Edgar will ruff the third diamond, but he cannot harm you. If he returns a trump, you simply win and continue diamonds. If he switches to a club, you win, cross to the ♠A and again can continue playing diamonds. Finally, if he continues hearts, you ruff and continue diamonds. All ways on, you retain control.

Win the Big Match

South (You)
♠ Q 7 4
♡ K Q
♢ Q J 10 2
♣ A K Q J

After Edgar passes, your opening bid presents no problem: 2NT. Pat responds with a 3♢ transfer, showing five or more hearts, and you obediently rebid 3♡. Pat now calls 3NT, offering a choice of games. The heart holding suggests playing in hearts to overcome a possible blockage, but other factors point to 3NT. For one, you might have four top losers in 4♡; for another, the defenders might be able to take ace, king and a ruff in spades or diamonds; for a third, your hand has the playing strength to give hope of making 3NT without the long hearts. So you pass.

West	North	East	South
Steve	*Pat*	*Edgar*	*You*
		Pass	2NT
Pass	3♢	Pass	3♡
Pass	3NT	All Pass	

West leads the ♢7 and East plays king, ace and, a little more hesitatingly, a third diamond.

♠ J 8 3
♡ A 9 8 5 3
♢ 9 4
♣ 10 9 4

♠ Q 7 4
♡ K Q
♢ Q J 10 2
♣ A K Q J

Winning the third diamond, how do you plan the play?

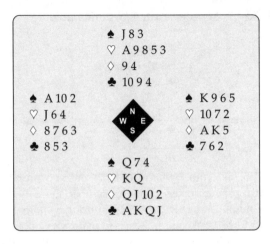

Evidently, Edgar was hoping the lead was fourth highest from a suit something like Q-10-8-7-x rather than second best from small cards. The play to the first three tricks has suited you anyway, whatever his motives. You now have nine tricks – except you cannot get to them all.

A doubleton ♡J-10 would see you home, but this sounds very much a long shot. Perhaps spades will produce a trick. If the ace and king lie in the same hand, you can set up a winner by force. Sadly, the odds on this have gone down as a result of the bidding and early play. Edgar, who passed as dealer, cannot have ace-king in two suits. Steve could have both top spades but, if he has any sort of length with them, then surely he would have led a spade in preference to a diamond. The fact that you have enough winners but not the entries to cash them may suggest a stepping-stone squeeze, and this is surely the thing to try; you will normally be able to guess what the defenders are keeping.

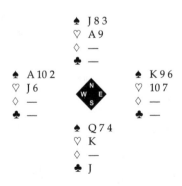

If you like, you can 'run' the ♡Q to see what happens, then cash all your winners in the minors, keeping two spades in dummy. What can the defenders do? Someone needs to keep two hearts, or (assuming you read the position) you can overtake the ♡K with the ace. If West does, you have a choice of ways to make your ninth trick. It is more testing if East protects hearts. Then you cash the ♡K and duck a spade, scoring the ♡A (or the ♠Q) on the last trick.

BOARD 35   Dealer: South. E/W Vulnerable.

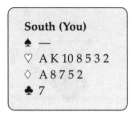

> **South (You)**
> ♠ —
> ♡ A K 10 8 5 3 2
> ◊ A 8 7 5 2
> ♣ 7

Some believe in pre-empting at every available opportunity, taking the view that forcing the others to guess will embarrass two opponents but only one partner. I am not sure I wholly agree with this philosophy. On a hand like this, you have three possible quick defensive winners and you expect that their trump suit will break badly. Moreover, you risk missing a slam if you pre-empt. These cards offer play for a slam facing the right Yarborough (e.g. give partner a 5-4-1-3 distribution). Steve doubles your 1♡ opening and Edgar jumps to 2♠. Now you must decide whether to bother showing your second suit. Let us say you do, and Steve jumps to 4♠ over your 3◊, making this the auction:

West	North	East	South
Steve	*Pat*	*Edgar*	*You*
			1♡
Dbl	Pass	2♠	3◊
4♠	All Pass		

You lead the ♡A and dummy comes down. 'Thank you very much, partner,' Edgar says.

> ♠ K Q 10 9
> ♡ Q 6
> ◊ K J
> ♣ A Q J 10 3
>
> ♠ —
> ♡ A K 10 8 5 3 2
> ◊ A 8 7 5 2
> ♣ 7

You cash the ♡K at trick two, as all follow and your partner completes a high-low, seven and then four. How should you continue?

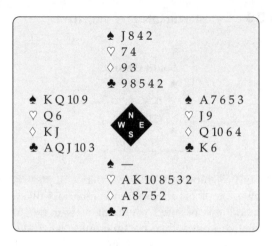

You have made two tricks and feel optimistic about scoring a third with the ◇A. Where should you look for a fourth?

If partner has the ◇Q, a low diamond switch could put declarer to a guess. Unfortunately, it is one he appears almost certain to get right. Given that you have bid twice whilst North has passed throughout, which defender would you place with the ◇A if you were in his shoes?

Room just about exists for partner to hold the ♣K. If so, you need do nothing special. You can just cash your ◇A and wait for a club trick to come. Can you spot any other chances?

Declarer could have only four trumps, so be running into a 5-0 split. If he has four clubs as well, any continuation will defeat the contract but, if he has three clubs, your only chance is to play a third round of hearts in the hope that Pat has the ♠J; then Edgar would need to take an inspired view to make the contract.

Surely, finding ♠J-8-x-x opposite represents your most realistic hope, or at any rate one for which you should cater. Left to his own devices, declarer can cash the ♠K first and pick up such a holding via a marked finesse. Fortunately, partner, if given the chance, can make a pre-emptive strike. You need to cash the ◇A and play a third round of hearts. If dummy ruffs, Pat discards. If not, ruffing with the ♠8 will force out the ace. True, giving a ruff and discard may cost if declarer is missing the ♣K (and has exactly two clubs), but then you have to ask yourself why, with no desire for a heart continuation, partner would choose to play high-low in hearts.

Win the Big Match

BOARD 36

Dealer: West. Game All.

South (You)
- ♠ A K Q J 9 6 4
- ♡ Q
- ◇ K 4
- ♣ A J 6

After two passes, Edgar opens 1♡. To overcall 3♡, asking partner to bid 3NT with a heart stopper is one option, albeit an inflexible one. Some people play that 4♡ here shows a strong 4♠ overcall, but you dismiss this on two counts: (a) you do not recall discussing this with Pat and (b) the hand seems a bit too good. So you double. Steve jumps to 3♡ and this comes back round. Jumping to 3♠ would express your values nicely, but you cannot do that (and it would be highly unethical to pull out a 'stop' card before bidding 3♠). Your 4♠ ends the bidding.

West	North	East	South
Steve	*Pat*	*Edgar*	*You*
Pass	Pass	1♡	Dbl
3♡	Pass	Pass	4♠
All Pass			

West leads the ♡2 and Edgar wins with the king. He continues with the ♡A. Can you find a route to ten tricks?

- ♠ 10 7
- ♡ 7 5 4
- ◇ 9 8 6 5 2
- ♣ 10 9 7

- ♠ A K Q J 9 6 4
- ♡ Q
- ◇ K 4
- ♣ A J 6

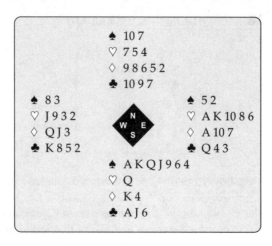

```
              ♠ 10 7
              ♡ 7 5 4
              ◇ 9 8 6 5 2
              ♣ 10 9 7
 ♠ 8 3                        ♠ 5 2
 ♡ J 9 3 2        N           ♡ A K 10 8 6
 ◇ Q J 3      W       E       ◇ A 10 7
 ♣ K 8 5 2        S           ♣ Q 4 3
              ♠ A K Q J 9 6 4
              ♡ Q
              ◇ K 4
              ♣ A J 6
```

Hardly unexpectedly, given that the vulnerable opponents have bid to the three level, Pat's hand contains no picture cards. Luckily, it does include a couple of tens, and these may prove vital.

You count eight sure tricks, and finding a ninth should not prove too taxing. The ♠10 represents a sure entry, and if you use it to lead up to the ◇K and the opening bidder has the ◇A then the ◇K will score. Of course, if you do that, you will almost certainly lose two clubs.

Several possible ways exist to overcome the entry problem, and the right one depends upon how you view the club layout. So do you think East has the king-queen? You have already seen ace-king of hearts in his hand, and you have to assume that he has the ◇A to give you a chance. If he has 5 points in clubs, this gives him a minimum of 16. With at least 16 points Edgar might have opened a strong no-trump (if balanced) or gone to 4♡ (if he has a bit of shape). Besides, holding at most 4 points, Steve's vulnerable jump raise would be adventurous, certainly by the standards of solid rubber bridge players.

Might it help to find East with ♣K-x or ♣Q-x? In this case, if you cross to the ♠10, play a club to the jack and it loses, the ♣10 will provide an entry for leading diamonds. Sadly, the defenders have two ways to thwart this: either East plays high or West lets your jack hold. At the risk of looking silly, your best shot must be to try for a second entry to dummy by ruffing the heart high and finessing the ♠7. If this works, you play a club to the jack, planning to run the ♣10 later. Assuming reasonable breaks, this will give you an entry for leading diamonds as well.

BOARD 37   Dealer: North. N/S Vulnerable.

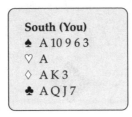

South (You)
- ♠ A 10 9 6 3
- ♡ A
- ◊ A K 3
- ♣ A Q J 7

In third seat, you open 2♣, the system strong bid. Pat responds 2◊, which normally denies 8 points or more. You rebid 2♠ and Pat jumps to 4♠. Mike Lawrence is right when he says that a jump bid in a forcing situation should have a special (and useful) meaning, and here you play it to indicate good trumps but poor controls. You could bid 4NT to find out whether Pat has the ♠K or the ♠Q (possibly both), but this will not locate a third-round diamond control (when the slam may depend on one of two finesses). Given that you have fair play for a slam facing a 5-3-3-2 Yarborough, you bite the bullet and jump to 6♠.

West	North	East	South
Steve	*Pat*	*Edgar*	*You*
	Pass	Pass	2♣
Pass	2◊	Pass	2♠
Pass	4♠	Pass	6♠
All Pass			

West leads the ♡J and dummy puts down about what you expected. 'I hope this is enough,' Pat comments.

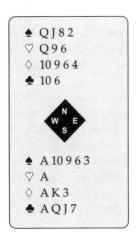

♠ Q J 8 2
♡ Q 9 6
◊ 10 9 6 4
♣ 10 6

♠ A 10 9 6 3
♡ A
◊ A K 3
♣ A Q J 7

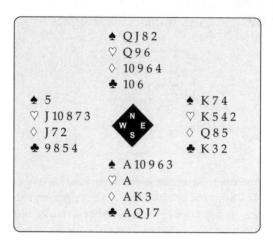

```
              ♠ Q J 8 2
              ♡ Q 9 6
              ◇ 10 9 6 4
              ♣ 10 6
♠ 5                           ♠ K 7 4
♡ J 10 8 7 3      N           ♡ K 5 4 2
◇ J 7 2        W     E        ◇ Q 8 5
♣ 9 8 5 4         S           ♣ K 3 2
              ♠ A 10 9 6 3
              ♡ A
              ◇ A K 3
              ♣ A Q J 7
```

Entry difficulties seem to be a theme on this set, but do not look for sympathy. The others would like to hold hands with 20 or more points!

If you could lead from dummy, you would finesse in spades and, if that fails, fall back on the club finesse, giving roughly 75% odds. Needless to say, deliberately leading out of the wrong hand would be unethical; in any event, you would stand little chance of getting away with it!

Suppose you lay down the ♠A. If the king falls, you can relax; if not, you are in big trouble. Even with the ♣K onside, you face a grave danger of losing a diamond trick. You might survive if East is 2-6-2-3 and holds the ♠K, as then you can cash two diamonds before playing a second trump to leave him endplayed. This is long odds against.

Playing ace and another club does not sound promising either. You stand little hope either of felling the ♣K or of being able to play four rounds of the suit (for dummy to throw two diamonds) without running into a ruff. Of course, if you ruff a winning club to take the trump finesse, you will (unless someone has ◇Q-J bare) lose a diamond.

Starting with a low club to the ten stands a slightly greater chance of success. West just might hold the king and duck. However, surely your best chance lies in attacking clubs with the queen or jack. Whoever holds the ♣K will need to take it or lose it. Then you will have the ♣10 as an entry to take the trump finesse. If this works and trumps do not break 4-0 (or West has an improbable 0-7-3-3 shape), you will be able to ruff a diamond in dummy later. True, if East has a doubleton club and someone holds up the ♣K (or clubs are 6-1 or worse), this will not work, but you cannot have everything.

BOARD 38   Dealer: East. E/W Vulnerable.

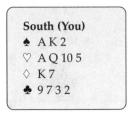

South (You)
♠ A K 2
♡ A Q 10 5
◊ K 7
♣ 9 7 3 2

Edgar opens 1◊ and it is your turn. Agreed, you have a balanced hand and a diamond stopper, but a take-out double describes the hand much better than 1NT. With a doubleton in the suit opened, you rate to belong in a suit contract unless partner is able to suggest otherwise. Steve bids 1♠, Pat competes with 2♣ and Edgar passes. You might have doubled on less than this, and without four clubs. So, given that Pat bid 2♣ freely, you feel justified in raising. You half expect 3♣ to buy the contract, but Steve goes on to 3♠ to complete the bidding:

West	North	East	South
Steve	Pat	Edgar	You
		1◊	Dbl
1♠	2♣	Pass	3♣
3♠	All Pass		

Pat leads the ♣K and you like the look of dummy. The king-jack of hearts under your ace-queen and the ◊A in front of your king suggest that the cards sit well for your side.

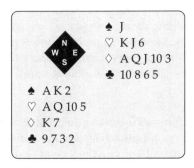

♠ J
♡ K J 6
◊ A Q J 10 3
♣ 10 8 6 5

♠ A K 2
♡ A Q 10 5
◊ K 7
♣ 9 7 3 2

Declarer wins the opening lead with the ace and, after silencing his mobile which has embarrassingly sprung to life, advances the ♠Q. How should you defend?

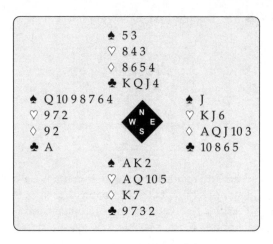

Clearly, the ♣A is a singleton, as Pat would not introduce a three-card club suit. Equally, declarer must possess strong trump intermediates, for otherwise he would not crash the queen and jack together. Since he bid to 3♠, vulnerable, with only 6 points, you can also place him with seven trumps. (You cannot beat the contract if he has eight).

This being the case, you can foresee what will happen if you defend on straightforward lines. Steve ruffs the club return, drives out your other spade winner and subsequently takes the diamond finesse. Having won with the king, you cannot get partner on play and can do no better than to cash the ♡A to stop the overtrick.

Do I hear you saying: 'Why not duck the first diamond smoothly? Then if declarer has a doubleton and repeats the finesse, he will be cut off from dummy.' If you think of nothing else, the idea sounds worth trying. The trouble is that the bidding strongly suggests you have the ◊K. Without it, you would have only 13-14 points, a flat shape (you would overcall 1♡ with a 3-5-1-4 shape) and modest club support for your raise to 3♣. Moreover, with 8 or 9 points and a diamond stopper, Pat might have bid 1NT over 1♠.

Fortunately, a sure-fire way exists to defeat the contract if Steve does have a doubleton diamond (in a 7-3-2-1 shape). Win the first spade and return a diamond! You will also win the second round of spades and play a diamond. With no further entry to dummy, declarer will attempt to cash a third round of diamonds, but you will ruff. Having overruffed, he may try running some trumps. If so, you keep A-Q-10 of hearts and a club with which to exit.

BOARD 39   Dealer: South. Game All.

> **South (You)**
> ♠ A K 10 2
> ♡ K Q 9 6 3
> ◇ 5
> ♣ J 9 3

You open 1♡, Pat responds 1♠ and Edgar overcalls 2◇. Without the overcall, you would have raised to 3♠, the standard way to describe a six-loser hand with four-card support for partner. Should you do the same now? I think the answer is yes. To jump all the way to 4♠ or to make a splinter of 4◇ would show a better hand than you have. You would risk conceding a penalty if the response was on a minimum with only four trumps. Also, overbidding increases the risk that partner will misjudge at the five level if Steve bids 5◇. Over 3♠, Steve bids 4◇, Pat goes on to 4♠ and Edgar, joining in the party, proceeds to 5◇.

You have bid your hand already and it would be rash to take a decision in front of partner. As far as you know, both sides have bid with a hope (or even expectation) of making their contracts, so this is not a 'forcing pass' situation. Pat clearly agrees, as 5◇ becomes the final contract.

West	North	East	South
Steve	*Pat*	*Edgar*	*You*
			1♡
Pass	1♠	2◇	3♠
4◇	4♠	5◇	All Pass

You lead the ♠A, which holds as partner plays the three and declarer the jack. How do you continue?

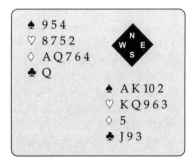

♠ 9 5 4
♡ 8 7 5 2
◇ A Q 7 6 4
♣ Q

♠ A K 10 2
♡ K Q 9 6 3
◇ 5
♣ J 9 3

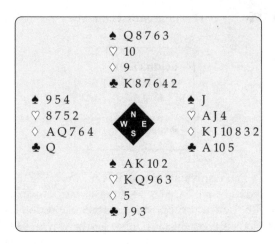

```
                    ♠ Q 8 7 6 3
                    ♡ 10
                    ◊ 9
                    ♣ K 8 7 6 4 2
   ♠ 9 5 4                        ♠ J
   ♡ 8 7 5 2          N           ♡ A J 4
   ◊ A Q 7 6 4    W       E       ◊ K J 10 8 3 2
   ♣ Q              S              ♣ A 10 5
                    ♠ A K 10 2
                    ♡ K Q 9 6 3
                    ◊ 5
                    ♣ J 9 3
```

You have scored a spade trick and can reasonably hope to make a heart trick. (A void with declarer is impossible on the bidding and, if he has a bare ♡A, you stand little hope of beating the contract). Where can the vital third defensive trick come from?

To have enough to bid 4♠, vulnerable, yet evidently insufficient to double 5◊, Pat must have a shapely hand, no doubt with a five-card spade suit. This tells you to discount the chance of a second spade winner. Besides, Pat might have played a higher spade with four.

Chances of a trump trick appear equally slim. Edgar can hardly have bid the way he has with jack to five. So, the only way of getting a trump trick will be if (a) Pat has the bare king and (b) declarer decides to take the finesse. For sure, Pat may have the ♣A and this represents your best prospect. What alternatives come to mind?

The ♡A should do it, but maybe another route could bring two heart tricks. If declarer has either ♡A-J-4, or ♡A-10-4, you must be in with the chance. A danger exists, however, and you need to spot it. Suppose Edgar has a 1-3-6-3 shape and you switch to a trump. Declarer wins in either hand, plays the ♣A (he must have this or the contract will fail anyway) and another club, then cross-ruffs the black suits (or he could ruff a spade first). Then, having completed the strip, he ducks a heart. If you do not win the trick, Pat will be obliged to concede a ruff and discard. If you do win the heart, you will have to crash partner's singleton and be equally stuck. To avoid this scenario (or a similar one if partner has a singleton ♡A and no ♣K), you must switch to the ♡K at trick two. This will fail if Edgar has ♡A-J-10 and the ♣A, but then nothing works.

BOARD 40   Dealer: West. Love All.

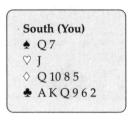

South (You)
♠ Q 7
♡ J
◇ Q 10 8 5
♣ A K Q 9 6 2

Steve opens 1♠ and Edgar responds 1NT. Your first move seems obvious. You would want 5-5 in the minors to start with an unusual 2NT, so you overcall 2♣. Steve rebids 2♡ and two passes follow this. To sell out at any vulnerability looks like a mistake. The opponents probably possess an eight-card fit, in which case you do not want to defend at the two level. You could bid an inflexible 3♣, or give partner some alternatives with double or 2NT. The hand really contains too few defensive values to double; also double fails to get across the four-card diamond suit. Pat removes 2NT to 3♣ and this ends the auction.

West	North	East	South
Steve	*Pat*	*Edgar*	*You*
1♠	Pass	1NT	2♣
2♡	Pass	Pass	2NT
Pass	3♣	All Pass	

West cashes two top spades, all following, then takes the ♡A before leading a third spade. East, who has played high-low with the jack and the six, ruffs with the ♣10. What is your plan?

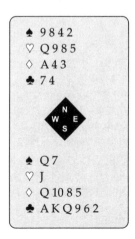

♠ 9 8 4 2
♡ Q 9 8 5
◇ A 4 3
♣ 7 4

♠ Q 7
♡ J
◇ Q 10 8 5
♣ A K Q 9 6 2

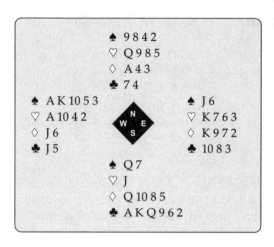

You have lost three tricks already and are bound to lose a diamond, so you must overruff now and hope the ♣J will drop in one or two rounds.

The real problem lies in restricting your losses in diamonds to one. Since West has turned up with the ace-king of spades and the ♡A, you can reasonably assume that Edgar, for his 1NT response, has the red kings. Given that Steve has promised at least nine cards in the majors you would, if you had the entries, play Edgar for the ♢J as well. As you do not, you will have to think of something else. Edgar would hardly have ruffed the spade from an initial trump holding of 10-8-5-3, which means you can discount any hope of a 3-3 diamond break. Indeed, when you draw trumps, both opponents follow to two rounds.

One possibility, if hearts are 5-3, is that Steve has a bare ♢J. Then you can cross to the ♢A and finesse the eight on the way back.

Given that Steve might have bid 3♡ over 3♣ with 5-5, the bare ♢J is unlikely. ♢J-9 doubleton sounds a better chance, but you can actually do it if Steve has the jack and any small diamond. You can cash all but one of your trumps and then lead the ♢Q from hand. If Edgar wins with the king, the ace drops the jack on the second round and you finesse the eight on the third. If he ducks, it comes to the much same thing.

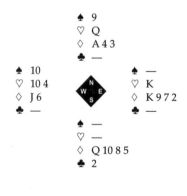

RESULTS ON BOARDS 33-40

Chris and Alex, who have just played East-West in the other room, enter yours. They finished a bit late, so you move straight to scoring.

On Board 33, the bidding also began: pass-pass-1♢-1♡-double, but Chris bid a pre-emptive 3♡. Suzanne jumped to 4♠ and Alex, perhaps hoping to avoid a double and forgetting Chris might have four spades, saved in 5♡. Lucy did double, though, and collected 300. This means you gain 3 IMPs if you made 4♠, lose 10 if you went three down (if you took two top trumps and omitted to take a heart ruff once you knew three diamonds would not stand up), lose 9 for two down or 8 for one down.

On Board 34, Suzanne also played in 3NT on a diamond attack. She unblocked the ♡K-Q and led the ♠Q, pretending that she held ♠K-Q-x and wanted dummy's ♠J as an entry. Alex, West, did not fall for this and won with the ace, the clue having come on the second heart: East, Chris, played the ♡10 as a suit-preference signal for spades. You gain 12 IMPs if you made 3NT; the board is flat if not.

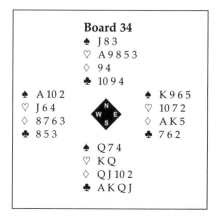

Board 34
- ♠ J 8 3
- ♡ A 9 8 5 3
- ♢ 9 4
- ♣ 10 9 4

- ♠ A 10 2
- ♡ J 6 4
- ♢ 8 7 6 3
- ♣ 8 5 3

- ♠ K 9 6 5
- ♡ 10 7 2
- ♢ A K 5
- ♣ 7 6 2

- ♠ Q 7 4
- ♡ K Q
- ♢ Q J 10 2
- ♣ A K Q J

On Board 35, Suzanne could not resist opening 4♡ with your hand. Alex, West, doubled and Chris took the double out to 4♠. Suzanne also cashed two hearts. At trick three, paths diverged, as she switched to a low diamond, a fair shot. In practice, Chris had no guess and 4♠ made. This gives you the chance to gain 12 IMPs by beating 4♠; the board is flat if it made.

South (Suzanne)
- ♠ —
- ♡ A K 10 8 5 3 2
- ♢ A 8 7 5 2
- ♣ 7

True to form, on Board 36, Suzanne doubled and then bid 4♠. Alex attacked with the ♢Q, and then something clever happened. Winning with the ace, Chris played the ace and then a low heart. Fooled about the location of the ♡K, declarer thought she might find ♣K-Q onside, so did not bother finessing the ♠7. This means you win 12 IMPs if you made 4♠ or lose 3 if you went two down; one down gives a flat board.

On Board 37 you were in a thin slam and the news that Suzanne and Lucy stayed out of it comes as no surprise. In consequence, you gain or lose 13 IMPs depending upon whether you made 6♠ or went down.

On Board 38 the bidding took a different turn in the other room, as Alex and Chris play US-style weak jump shifts after an intervening take-out double. This gadget worked well, as Alex got to play in 2♠. Naturally, Suzanne did not shift to a diamond, and an overtrick resulted. This means you gain 6 IMPs if you beat 3♠; if you let through an overtrick (making the ◇K but not the ♡A), the cost is 1 IMP and you lose 2 if you allowed eleven tricks (ducking the ◇K); nine tricks gives a flat board.

On Board 39, the other players misjudged. The auction got to 5◇ more rapidly and Lucy went on to 5♠. Often, if you push your opponents from four of a major to five of it, there is no need to double, since you score well if they go one down, and that was the philosophy Chris adopted as East. Regrettably, as even 4♠ was failing and 5◇ stood some chance of making, a double would have worked a treat.

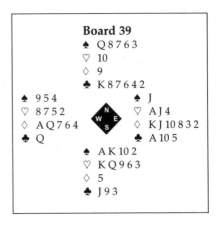

Board 39

♠ Q 8 7 6 3
♡ 10
◇ 9
♣ K 8 7 6 4 2

♠ 9 5 4
♡ 8 7 5 2
◇ A Q 7 6 4
♣ Q

♠ J
♡ A J 4
◇ K J 10 8 3 2
♣ A 10 5

♠ A K 10 2
♡ K Q 9 6 3
◇ 5
♣ J 9 3

As it was, they collected 300, by taking 5♠ undoubled three down. Alex won the diamond lead and switched to the ♣Q. Two club ruffs and three aces gave the defenders five tricks in all. This result means you gain 9 IMPs if you beat 5◇ or lose 7 if you allowed it to make.

Again, on Board 40, more bidding took place at the other table than at yours. For no real reason (other than that neither side vulnerable is a good time for declaring competitive part-score deals, as anyone going down does so in 50s), Chris and Alex pushed on to 3♡, going one down. So, you gain 2 IMPs if you made 3♣ or lose 3 if you went down.

Although you have passed halfway, the end still seems some distance away. You are reconciled now to the fact that you will play throughout. For the sixth set, you will face Wayne and Sally in the open room, as Lucy and Suzanne intend to take a break. In the closed room, Sam and Phil will play against Edgar and Steve.

Win the Big Match

BOARD 41   Dealer: North. E/W Vulnerable.

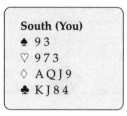

South (You)
♠ 9 3
♡ 9 7 3
◇ A Q J 9
♣ K J 8 4

Pat opens 3♡ and Sally doubles for take-out. With heart support and these values, you intend to take some positive action. What should it be? You could make a case for bidding either minor, to direct the lead if Wayne plays in a spade contract, and perhaps to help partner judge whether to go to the five level. The diamonds are stronger than the clubs, but not by a decisive amount. Rather than guess wrongly which minor to show, and give the opponents extra information and bidding space at the same time, you simply raise to 4♡. Wayne bids 4♠ and you pass this out. You have too much strength in the minors sitting over the take-out doubler to accept a minus by bidding 5♡.

West	North	East	South
Wayne	*Pat*	*Sally*	*You*
	3♡	Dbl	4♡
4♠	All Pass		

Pat leads the ♡K. 'You picked the right suit,' Sally says as she puts down her five-card support. 'Looks great,' Wayne replies, but you see that the cards lie well for your side:

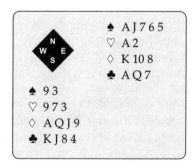

Winning with the ace in dummy, declarer ruffs a heart, draws trumps in two rounds (Pat follows once before discarding a low heart) and then leads the ◇3 to the five, ten and jack. What do you return?

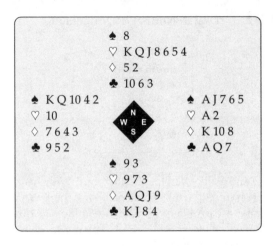

You have a count on the majors but cannot be quite so sure about declarer's lengths in the minors. With the ◇4 and ◇2 both missing, it looks like Pat's five is the start of a high-low, signifying a doubleton, though a holding of 7-6-5 remains just possible.

You will have to make a losing lead now, either playing round to one of dummy's tenaces or by conceding a ruff and discard. The secret is to avoid having to make a second losing lead. If we take the most likely situation, that Wayne is 5-1-4-3, let us consider each option in turn.

Suppose you lead a heart. Wayne ruffs in hand, discarding a diamond from dummy, then puts you in with the ◇A. You can exit safely with a diamond but, after ruffing this in dummy, declarer comes to hand with a trump and plays a fourth diamond, dummy throwing a club. With only clubs left, you must lead into dummy's A-Q. You suffer a similar fate if, at tricks six and seven,

you play ace and another diamond. In this case, winning with the king in dummy, declarer crosses to hand with a trump and executes the same loser-on-loser play.

Your only chance lies in leading a club, and you have to hope Pat has the ten, else you will be thrown back in with third round of clubs. Indeed, to ensure partner wins the third club, you must lead the king or jack now.

> **South (You)**
> ♠ J 10 7 3
> ♡ K 7 6 5
> ◇ 10
> ♣ J 10 8 3

Sally opens 3♡, you pass, Wayne raises to 4♡ and Pat doubles. What do you bid? Despite the level, the double still asks for take-out, though one is aware that four tricks are often easier to score than ten or eleven. Pat should have at least spade tolerance (or great strength) and 4♠ may be cold. However, spades will often be a 4-4 fit and, even if Pat is void, the opponents have only nine hearts. On the Law of Total Tricks, this means that 4♡ doubled might net 800 if 4♠ is makeable, so you pass.

West	North	East	South
Wayne	*Pat*	*Sally*	*You*
		3♡	Pass
4♡	Dbl	All Pass	

The real decision is the lead. With four trumps, you usually do not lead a singleton. Here declarer is marked with long trumps, however, and you may have time to try a diamond later. If you lead a black suit, the textbooks all say it is better (both safer and more attacking) to lead from J-10 if you have the nine or eight as well, so you go for the ♣J.

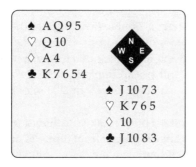

> ♠ A Q 9 5
> ♡ Q 10
> ◇ A 4
> ♣ K 7 6 5 4
>
>   ♠ J 10 7 3
>   ♡ K 7 6 5
>   ◇ 10
>   ♣ J 10 8 3

Declarer ruffs the club, then plays ace and another diamond, on which you discard a club. Pat, who played the ◇6 first time, wins the second with the ◇Q and shifts to a trump. Sally plays low and your king wins. How do you continue?

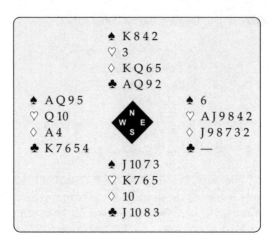

```
              ♠ K 8 4 2
              ♡ 3
              ◇ K Q 6 5
              ♣ A Q 9 2
  ♠ A Q 9 5              ♠ 6
  ♡ Q 10      N          ♡ A J 9 8 4 2
  ◇ A 4     W   E        ◇ J 9 8 7 3 2
  ♣ K 7 6 5 4   S        ♣ —
              ♠ J 10 7 3
              ♡ K 7 6 5
              ◇ 10
              ♣ J 10 8 3
```

Declarer has played on dummy's short suit and you have the chance to remove dummy's final trump. Should you take it?

To resolve that question, you should consider a couple of others:

(a) Why has Sally, who is vulnerable and playing weak two bids, opened 3♡ on an indifferent six-card suit?

(b) If only a trump continuation can defeat the contract, why did declarer allow you to win the first round of trumps?

The answer to (a) must be that Sally has a 'strawberry jam' hand – lots of red cards. What you can see and the knowledge that Pat (who you know has a minimum double) must have some spades confirms this.

The fact that the contract is doubled complicates the answer to (b). True, if declarer just needed a diamond ruff to make the contract, she would have grabbed the ♡A and taken the ruff. However, maybe she needed the trump finesse *and* a ruff (for example if she is 2-6-5-0 with ◇J-8-x-x-x), meaning a trump return might transform 200 into 500.

A 6-6 shape occurs rarely, but I think you should play for one here. For the ◇6 not be the start of a high-low from four, Pat must have begun with ◇K-Q-8-7-6 or better. If that were the layout, Sally might well have won the first heart to ensure one ruff. As the cards lie, it proves essential for you to play a forcing game, persevering with clubs. This way, upon getting in with the ◇K, Pat will be able either to cash the ♣A (if declarer draws trumps) or to continue the force (if she does not).

BOARD 43   Dealer: South. Love All.

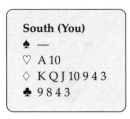

South (You)
♠ —
♡ A 10
◊ K Q J 10 9 4 3
♣ 9 8 4 3

As dealer, you consider your options. You and Pat do not play South African Texas (or 'Namyats' as it is known in the US), so you could open 1◊, 3◊, 4◊ or 5◊. Non-vulnerable, a 3◊ pre-empt surely does not do justice to the hand. 1◊ reflects the values more – and the fact that potentially your hand contains two defensive tricks. Of course, 1◊ does nothing to make life difficult for the opposing side or convey to partner your playing strength. With only seven sure playing tricks, 5◊ sounds too much, which leaves you with 4◊. Without taking too big a risk, this gets across your big distribution, and it leaves the opponents enough rope with which to hang themselves. Pat raises to game.

West	North	East	South
Wayne	Pat	Sally	You
			4◊
Pass	5◊	All Pass	

West leads the ♠K, which on their methods promises one or both of the ace and queen. How you do plan the play?

♠ J 10 5
♡ Q J 7
◊ A 8 6
♣ K Q 5 2

♠ —
♡ A 10
◊ K Q J 10 9 4 3
♣ 9 8 4 3

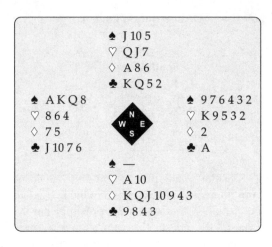

```
            ♠ J 10 5
            ♡ Q J 7
            ◇ A 8 6
            ♣ K Q 5 2
♠ A K Q 8                    ♠ 9 7 6 4 3 2
♡ 8 6 4         N            ♡ K 9 5 3 2
◇ 7 5        W   E           ◇ 2
♣ J 10 7 6      S            ♣ A
            ♠ —
            ♡ A 10
            ◇ K Q J 10 9 4 3
            ♣ 9 8 4 3
```

You see a possible heart loser (if West has the king), one certain club loser (the ace) and, depending upon how the suit breaks, a second if not a third club loser. Clearly, you need something to sit kindly.

If West has the ♡K, you seem to have little choice about what to do; dummy's third-round heart winner will take care of one club and you will need to hope West has the ♣A or ♣J-10 bare. The play offers more scope if East has the ♡K. Now you succeed any time East has ♡K-x (or covers the ♡Q), or clubs split 3-2, or West has the ♣A, or if one of the ♣10 and ♣J is bare. Can you cope with other layouts?

If East has ♣A-J-10-x *and* you read the position, you can strip her exit cards via a squeeze and throw her in. You just draw trumps ending in dummy, take the heart finesse and run all but one trump. To keep four clubs and ♡K-x, East must throw her spades away. Then you can cash the ♡A and play a club. East can win and exit with the ♡K, but you ruff and run the ♣9. Sadly, this line means giving up on several other chances.

```
        ♠ J
        ♡ Q J
        ◇ —
        ♣ K Q 5 2
♠ A Q 8              ♠ 9
♡ 8 6 4      N      ♡ K 9
◇ —       W   E    ◇ —
♣ 7          S      ♣ A J 10 6
        ♠ —
        ♡ A
        ◇ Q 4
        ♣ 9 8 4 3
```

For practical purposes, the best you can do after drawing trumps is to take the heart finesse and, if it wins, cash the ♡A. Then, if the ♡K has not fallen and West follows low when you lead a club, dummy ducks! This picks up a bare ace offside without harming other prospects.

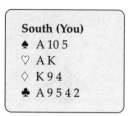

> **South (You)**
> ♠ A 10 5
> ♡ A K
> ◇ K 9 4
> ♣ A 9 5 4 2

After three passes, you can open 1♣ and Wayne overcalls 1♠. Pat doubles; this is a negative double, normally including four hearts. Sally passes and you must find a rebid. Since a 1NT opening would have shown 15-17 (yes, I know a case exists for playing weak in fourth seat), a 2NT jump rebid promises 18-19. If you cannot bear the thought of being left in 2NT, you could cue-bid 2♠ or, at the risk of suggesting a running club suit, jump to 3NT. Anyway, you call 2NT and Pat raises.

West	North	East	South
Wayne	*Pat*	*Sally*	*You*
Pass	Pass	Pass	1♣
1♠	Dbl	Pass	2NT
Pass	3NT	All Pass	

West leads the ♠K and East discourages with the three.

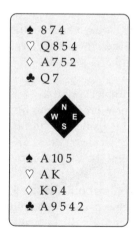

> ♠ 8 7 4
> ♡ Q 8 5 4
> ◇ A 7 5 2
> ♣ Q 7
>
>   N
>   W   E
>   S
>
> ♠ A 10 5
> ♡ A K
> ◇ K 9 4
> ♣ A 9 5 4 2

How do you plan the play?

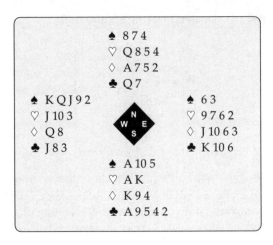

With only seven quick winners, you will need to do something with the clubs. Wayne might, you suppose, have overcalled on K-Q-J-x, but the odds seem against this. If he does have five spades, you will surely have to hope Sally has the ♣K. (Even if Wayne has three hearts and two diamonds, it does you no good to win the second spade, cash the red tops and exit in spades. Yes, he will have to lead a club but, unless dummy's ♡8 is now a winner, the ♣Q gives you only an eighth trick.)

Having decided you want Sally to hold the ♣K, your next wish may be for a 3-3 break, ideally with the jack on your right. Let us see what happens if you hold up the ♠A, and lead a club to the queen and king. Oops – Sally shifts to a low diamond. Where do you win this? If you take it in dummy to lead a club, you never get to the ♡Q. If, however, you win it in hand, unblock the hearts, cross to the ◇A and cash the ♡Q, you will kill all your entries to hand and create lots of fast losers.

You try again, this time unblocking the ♡A-K at tricks three and four. Now, provided Sally has no more than four hearts, you can succeed if she has ♣K-J-x. You can win the diamond switch in dummy, cash the ♡Q and lead a club. If she plays the jack, you duck; if not, you go up with the ace and give her the third round. Might you improve on this?

Yes, you can make the contract if Sally has ♣K-J-x or ♣K-10-x. To take advantage of the latter, you must tackle the clubs differently. At trick five, lead the nine, intending to run it. Wayne pops another mint and covers to prevent this, so you are forced to play dummy's queen after all. Now, though, when you lead a club towards the ace, you can let Sally win with her ten on whichever round she plays it.

BOARD 45   Dealer: North. Game All.

South (You)
♠ 8
♡ K 9 4
♢ A K 7
♣ A K Q J 10 5

Pat, North, opens 1♠ and East passes. Proceeding slowly will just store up problems and you respond 3♣. Pat rebids 3♠. You could bid 4♣ next, but it seems unclear what this will achieve. So you bid 4NT, Roman Key Card Blackwood. Pat makes the bid you want to hear, 5♣. Zero key cards are impossible, so this shows three: two aces, and the king of the last bid suit, spades. You ask about the ♠Q with 5♢ but Pat denies it. You can only count twelve tricks, but a major-suit jack or ♢J-10 will make 7♣ depend at worst on a finesse, whilst a queen or a doubleton in a red suit should make it cold. You take the plunge...

West	North	East	South
Wayne	*Pat*	*Sally*	*You*
	1♠	Pass	3♣
Pass	3♠	Pass	4NT
Pass	5♣	Pass	5♢
Pass	5♠	Pass	7♣
All Pass			

West leads the ♡J. How you do plan the play? Take your time.

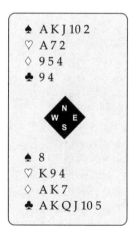

♠ A K J 10 2
♡ A 7 2
♢ 9 5 4
♣ 9 4

♠ 8
♡ K 9 4
♢ A K 7
♣ A K Q J 10 5

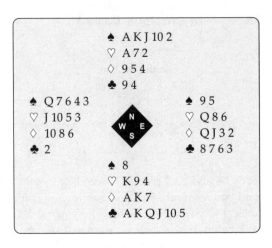

A spade finesse is an option, but a ruffing finesse seems superior, as it also picks up ♣Q-x with West. Luckily, thanks to the ♣9, you have a better play. By winning with the ♡K, and cashing just one trump, you have the entries to ruff two spades and succeed if spades are 4-3 (and trumps not 5-0) or someone has ♠Q-x. Can you improve even on this?

If West shows out when you ruff a spade, you will have a marked ruffing finesse, but you will need him to have only two trumps to take advantage. Wait a minute. If West is short in spades, he may have sole control of hearts, so you might dispense with the ruffing finesse, playing for a double squeeze instead. A squeeze should also work if he has five spades and you read the discards correctly. Difficult to see, perhaps, is that if West has five spades, you must cash the ace-king early (i.e. before ruffing a spade), discarding a heart. In the diagrammed position (below), your fifth trump squeezes West in three suits, and he no doubt keeps the ♠Q.

If he comes down to one heart, you play your last trump to remove his last heart and East, to keep two hearts, must come down to two diamonds. Crossing to the ♡A then squeezes West in diamonds and spades. If, at trick eight, he comes down to two diamonds, you can play your last trump and the top diamonds in either order. This will force East to release her heart guard, and then West is squeezed in the majors.

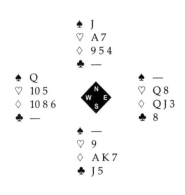

> **South (You)**
> ♠ 10 7 6 4 3
> ♡ A 3
> ◊ 10 3
> ♣ A K Q 8

Sally, East, opens 1♡ and you are next to call. Although you would prefer a better spade suit for overcalling 1♠, any other action would seriously misdescribe your hand. With this much in the way of playing strength, you can hardly pass; double, as well as risking an awkward 2◊ response, may lose a 5-3 spade fit. Pat cue bids 2♡, which you may recall guarantees spade support. You have more than you need for a simple overcall and must find a way of conveying this: you make the natural bid of 3♣; Pat closes the auction with a jump to 4♠.

West	North	East	South
Wayne	*Pat*	*Sally*	*You*
		1♡	1♠
Pass	2♡	Pass	3♣
Pass	4♠	All Pass	

West leads the ♡10 and, when you see the dummy, you notice that 3NT would have proved a safer spot. Perhaps Pat might have bid it over 3♣ to offer you the choice. Anyway, how can you make 4♠?

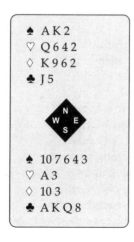

> ♠ A K 2
> ♡ Q 6 4 2
> ◊ K 9 6 2
> ♣ J 5
>
> ♠ 10 7 6 4 3
> ♡ A 3
> ◊ 10 3
> ♣ A K Q 8

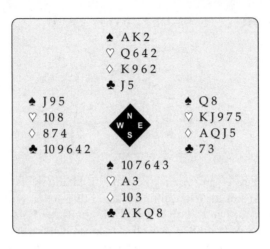

As Sally would have a strange 1♡ bid without the ◊A, you count four losers. ♠Q-J doubleton would solve all your problems, but this seems improbable. Most likely, you need a throw-in, so dummy plays low at trick one and you win with the ace. Then you cash the two top trumps. No miracle occurs, but everyone follows. To strip Sally's exit cards and to give the her a chance to err, you turn to clubs next, taking the jack first.

Sally is too good a player to ruff the third or fourth round of clubs (not that she can as the cards lie), but her discards may help you. You may also be able to tell from her tempo whether she could ruff. When you lead the third club, you must decide what to throw from dummy. If you believe that West has led a singleton or that Sally cannot get under his second heart, you could keep all dummy's hearts and try exiting with a heart. In practice this is against the odds and, after dummy discards a heart, the real crunch comes on the fourth club in the position below:

If you think that Sally holds the last trump, you discard a diamond from dummy and put her in with the trump. If you think Wayne does, dummy must throw a heart and you exit in hearts. As Wayne and Sally seem to have seven cards each between hearts and clubs, you may go by the fall of the trumps. Whoever contributed the queen or the jack on the second round is roughly twice as likely to have a doubleton as Q-J-x.

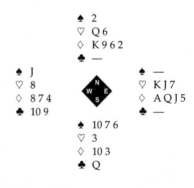

> **South (You)**
> ♠ A Q
> ♡ K J 10 7 3
> ◇ Q 10 6 5
> ♣ A 10

In response to your 1♡ opening, partner bids 2NT (Jacoby), showing game values and primary heart support. You rebid 3♡ (waiting and denying a singleton or void) and Pat bids 3♠ (first- or second-round control). You continue with 4♣ and Pat goes 4◇ (more 'Italian style' cue bids). Up until now, each of you may have shown your controls in case the other had extra values. This changes when you proceed with 4♠, which, as it takes the bidding above game, constitutes a real slam try. Pat thinks so, and jumps to 6♡. Your auction looks like this:

West	North	East	South
Wayne	*Pat*	*Sally*	*You*
			1♡
Pass	2NT	Pass	3♡
Pass	3♠	Pass	4♣
Pass	4◇	Pass	4♠
Pass	6♡	All Pass	

West leads the ♡9 (from 9-8-x). How you do plan the play?

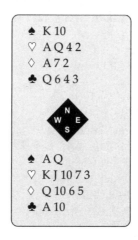

> ♠ K 10
> ♡ A Q 4 2
> ◇ A 7 2
> ♣ Q 6 4 3
>
> ♠ A Q
> ♡ K J 10 7 3
> ◇ Q 10 6 5
> ♣ A 10

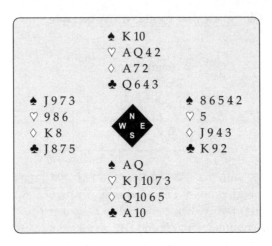

The hands fit poorly with two spades in each hand and the ♣Q wasted. You are going to need some luck here. West could hold a bare ◊K, solving all your problems, but this chance seems remote. Surely, you will need to arrange that the one trick in the minors you lose endplays the defender who wins it. What possibilities present themselves?

If you plan to exit in clubs and West wins (from K-x), you will need him to hold ◊K-x and to lead a diamond; a ruff and discard will do you no good. You are even less well placed if East wins. Instead, you must plan to find someone, ideally West, with ◊K-x. In case Sally has ◊K-x and the ♣K, you might as well win the trump lead in hand and play a diamond to the ace at trick two (she is less likely to unblock this early). Then you draw trumps, which takes two more rounds, and cash the ♠A and ♠K. If trumps were 2-2, you could afford to play a diamond to the ten. On the actual layout, you must duck the diamond completely.

West wins and, knowing a ruff and discard will be fatal, tries a low club. It looks like a 50-50 guess whether to put up the queen or let the lead run round to your hand. In fact, there is a slight reason to play low: Wayne cannot know who has the ◊10 and ♣10; if he had the ♣K, he just *might* have put up his ◊K at trick two, praying Sally had the ◊10. Of course, there will be no guess if it is East who wins the second diamond.

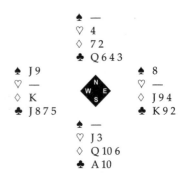

BOARD 48   Dealer: West. E/W Vulnerable.

South (You)
♠ K Q 9 8 2
♡ 10 9 3
◇ A 5
♣ 9 7 3

Fourth in hand, you hear Wayne open 1◇ (better minor, can be 4-4 but not 3-3) and Sally respond 1♠. 2♠ here would show spades, but it would also promise a rather better hand than this, so you pass. Wayne rebids 1NT (12-14 and usually balanced) and Sally raises to 3NT. Usually you pass when the opponents bid freely to game. Is that right here?

The cards may lie badly for declarer, with 3NT failing on any lead, but you must have a better chance to beat it on a spade lead. If a double transforms –600 into +200, you may gain 13 IMPs (if team-mates make 3NT in the other room on a non-spade lead), whilst transforming –600 into –750 would cost 4 IMPs. So, ignoring the possibility of overtricks or a redouble, a lead-directing double only needs to work more than four times in 17 to show a plus. In real life, the danger of a redouble or of overtricks cuts the odds slightly, but not enough to deter you.

West	North	East	South
Wayne	*Pat*	*Sally*	*You*
1◇	Pass	1♠	Pass
1NT	Pass	3NT	Dbl
All Pass			

Pat leads the ♠7 (presumably top of a doubleton) and dummy's ten is played. How do you proceed?

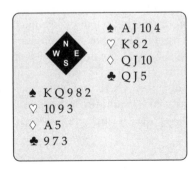

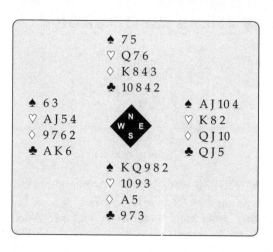

```
                    ♠ 7 5
                    ♡ Q 7 6
                    ◇ K 8 4 3
                    ♣ 10 8 4 2
  ♠ 6 3                              ♠ A J 10 4
  ♡ A J 5 4         N                ♡ K 8 2
  ◇ 9 7 6 2      W     E             ◇ Q J 10
  ♣ A K 6           S                ♣ Q J 5
                    ♠ K Q 9 8 2
                    ♡ 10 9 3
                    ◇ A 5
                    ♣ 9 7 3
```

Sally has quite a solid raise to 3NT, and she must have felt tempted to redouble, especially with the help she has in diamonds and the robust spade holding. Since you can see 23 points between your hand and dummy's, Pat can hold a maximum of 5 points on this deal. What could these consist of to give you a chance of beating the contract?

A heart holding of A-J-x-x sounds promising. Let us think this through. You win the spade, the ♡10 loses to the ♡K, you take the ◇A and lead a second heart. Is there a snag? Frankly, yes there is. Declarer can cover the ♡10 with the queen, forcing out the ace. If Pat continues with the ♡J, playing dummy's king will block the suit, whilst if Pat tries a low heart, declarer allows you to win with the nine. Nor does it help if Pat reverts to spades after the ♡A. In this case up goes dummy's ace and declarer has nine tricks after dislodging the ◇A.

It is even less good hoping for the ♣K and ♡Q opposite. If you win the spade and switch to a club then declarer can afford to let this run, as dummy's ♠A stands ready to deal with any switch back to spades.

By far your best chance lies in finding Pat with the ◇K (and the ♡Q as well, if Wayne has a four-card heart suit or, less likely, four clubs), though you need to spot the right timing to take advantage of this. If you win the first trick and return the suit, one stopper will remain in dummy and partner cannot continue the suit. The answer is to duck the first trick, encouraging with the nine. Then you will duck the first round of diamonds, allowing Pat to win and fire a spade through dummy's A-J-x. This way you get the spades set up while you still have the ◇A as an entry. Phew!

RESULTS ON BOARDS 41-48

'I am afraid they made a couple of fluky slams', says Sam on arriving at the table. 'However, we did make a doubled game', Phil adds.

On Board 41, the East hand offered a wide choice over the 3♡ pre-empt: 3♠, double and 3NT. Phil doubled, as Sally did, but, unlike you, Steve bid 4◇. This resulted in a diamond lead against 4♠, and two off, which means you lose 3 IMPs even if you beat 4♠; you lose 13 if you let it through.

East (Phil)
♠ A J 7 6 5
♡ A 2
◇ K 10 8
♣ A Q 7

You are grateful that the ♣8 persuaded you to lead a club against 4♡ doubled on Board 42, since at the other table Steve led the ♠J against the same contract, giving the defenders no chance. Team-mates' score of 790 means you win 13 IMPs if you beat 4♡ doubled; failing to do so produces a flat board.

On Board 43, when to make 5◇ you had to check you could afford a safety play in clubs, Sam played in 5♠ doubled after a 1◇ opening allowed Phil the chance to show both majors. On the ♣K lead, this might have made, but Edgar led the ◇A and shifted to a trump. Sam could now have escaped for only one down, by twice ducking a heart, but was unable to read the position. This gave North-South 300. This means you gain 3 IMPs if you made 5◇, or lose 8 if you did not.

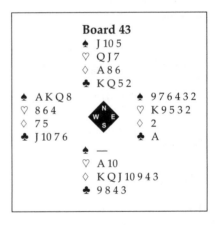

Board 43
♠ J 10 5
♡ Q J 7
◇ A 8 6
♣ K Q 5 2

♠ A K Q 8   ♠ 9 7 6 4 3 2
♡ 8 6 4   ♡ K 9 5 3 2
◇ 7 5   ◇ 2
♣ J 10 7 6   ♣ A

♠ —
♡ A 10
◇ K Q J 10 9 4 3
♣ 9 8 4 3

On Board 44, Steve was also in 3NT and spotted the need for making an avoidance play in clubs. He led the two, aiming to play dummy's seven, but Sam put in the eight.

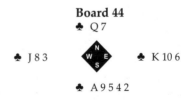

Board 44
♣ Q 7

♣ J 8 3   ♣ K 10 6

♣ A 9 5 4 2

So, the ♣J became an entry and Steve went two down. This means you gain 13 IMPs if you made 3NT or tie the board if you also lost 200.

Sometimes there is no justice! On Board 45 Steve and Edgar bid to the inferior contract of 7NT. Though he put off the crucial moment until quite late, Steve had little choice but to take the spade finesse to score 2220. At best, therefore, you lose 2 IMPs if you found the compound squeeze or took the straight finesse to make 7♣; you lose 20 if not.

On Board 46, when to make 4♠ you had to guess a defender's distribution, a different opening lead spared your counterpart the problem. Against Steve's 4♠, Sam led a diamond. This gave the defenders two diamonds but cost them their heart winner. So, you achieve a flat board if you found the right play to make 4♠. You lose 10 IMPs if you tried to exit in trumps or by ducking the second round of hearts.

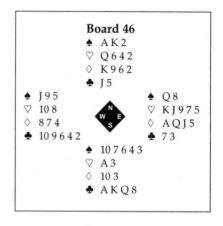

Board 46

♠ A K 2
♡ Q 6 4 2
◇ K 9 6 2
♣ J 5

♠ J 9 5   ♠ Q 8
♡ 10 8   ♡ K J 9 7 5
◇ 8 7 4   ◇ A Q J 5
♣ 10 9 6 4 2   ♣ 7 3

♠ 10 7 6 4 3
♡ A 3
◇ 10 3
♣ A K Q 8

How you do stay out of a slam with 31 points, all four aces and a solid 5-4 fit? Steve and Edgar cannot tell you. They also bid to 6♡ on Board 47. What is more, after a spade lead, Steve saw the need to play for a doubleton ◇K and, for the reason we discussed, put Sam with the ♣J. It is unlucky that the best dummy player in the opposing team sat South on this deal! Like it or lump it, the best you can do is to make 6♡ to flatten the board; you lose 17 IMPs if you went one or two down.

After three consecutive boards that offered no chance for a pick up (you need to prepare yourself for this when playing a good team), the news that Sam and Phil made 3NT (undoubled) on Board 48 after a club lead may come as a relief. You can win 13 IMPs if you defeated Wayne in 3NT doubled; your team loses 4 if you let him make it.

Team-mates achieved two good results, making 4♡ doubled on 42 and defeating 3NT on 44; otherwise, without doing anything really wrong, they did not fare so well. If you have gained IMPs on this particular set, you must have played well. Sam and Phil were due a rest for set seven anyway, and Chris and Alex will come in to replace them in the closed room against Lucy and Suzanne. Steve and Edgar, after their generally good set against Sam and Phil, will continue playing, but switch to doing so in the open room against you and Pat. At least Steve will have no chance to duplicate any of your heroics as declarer in this next set!

BOARD 49   Dealer: North. Love All.

```
                    South (You)
                    ♠ A 9 6
                    ♡ 3 2
                    ◊ J 9 5 2
                    ♣ 8 6 4 3
```

Pat, North, opens 1♠ and Edgar, East, passes. With some five-point hands, you would pass partner's opening bid (trade the ◊5 for the ♡5 and you might well do so, since then you would have an 11-loser hand). Here, with three-card support, an ace, a ruffing value (and a desire for a spade lead if West becomes declarer), a raise to 2♠ seems in order. You will, of course, decline any game try partner might make. In fact, this question does not arise, as Steve, West, overcalls 3♡ and Pat passes. Edgar goes on to 4♡ and this ends the auction:

West	North	East	South
Steve	*Pat*	*Edgar*	*You*
	1♠	Pass	2♠
3♡	Pass	4♡	All Pass

Pat leads the ♠5 and dummy comes down on your right.

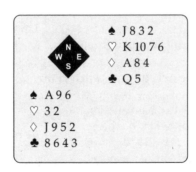

```
                         ♠ J 8 3 2
                         ♡ K 10 7 6
                         ◊ A 8 4
                         ♣ Q 5
              N
          W       E
              S
  ♠ A 9 6
  ♡ 3 2
  ◊ J 9 5 2
  ♣ 8 6 4 3
```

Declarer plays low from dummy and you win the first trick with the ace, the king falling on your left. This might be your one and only time on lead during the play. How do you make the most of it?

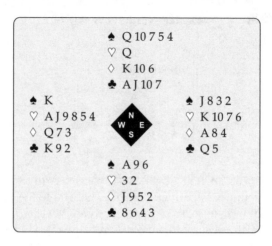

```
                 ♠ Q 10 7 5 4
                 ♡ Q
                 ◇ K 10 6
                 ♣ A J 10 7
 ♠ K                              ♠ J 8 3 2
 ♡ A J 9 8 5 4         N          ♡ K 10 7 6
 ◇ Q 7 3          W    E          ◇ A 8 4
 ♣ K 9 2              S           ♣ Q 5
                 ♠ A 9 6
                 ♡ 3 2
                 ◇ J 9 5 2
                 ♣ 8 6 4 3
```

You have scored one trick and, unless declarer is missing the ♡A or has a two-way finesse against the ♡Q and gets it wrong, you need to find three tricks in the minors. Pat would surely have led a top club from a suit headed by the ace-king despite your spade raise, which means your side probably needs to win two diamonds and a club.

If declarer has ♣K-J-x and ◇10-x-x then switching to a diamond may prove essential, and any card in the suit will do. If, however, he holds ♣A-J-x or ♣A-10-x, and ◇10-x-x then you must not lead the ◇J, as doing so would expose partner to an endplay.

Agreed, a diamond switch spares declarer a guess if he has ◇Q-10-x, but realistically he would never go wrong in view of the bidding and the fact that you have already turned up with ♠A. So, having decided that attacking diamonds is reasonably safe and may be necessary, and having ruled out leading the jack, do you switch to the ◇2?

The danger is that Pat has ◇K-10-x and the ♣A. Watch what happens. Knowing who has the ◇K, declarer allows the ten to win! Partner may get off play with a trump (or the ♣J), but declarer draws trumps, knocks out the ♣A and ruffs a club in dummy. He can also ruff a spade or two in hand, and finish the trumps to squeeze Pat in diamonds and spades. To thwart this line of play you should switch to the ◇9. If this holds, you continue the suit.

```
                 ♠ Q
                 ♡ —
                 ◇ K 6
                 ♣ —
 ♠ —                              ♠ J
 ♡ 8              N               ♡ —
 ◇ Q 7       W    E               ◇ A 8
 ♣ —             S                ♣ —
                 ♠ —
                 ♡ —
                 ◇ J 9
                 ♣ 8
```

Win the Big Match

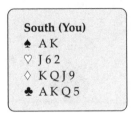

South (You)
♠ A K
♡ J 6 2
◇ K Q J 9
♣ A K Q 5

East, on your right passes, and you open 2♣. This is your system strong bid, 23+ if balanced. Pat responds 2NT, normally indicating 8-11 balanced. To convey the balanced nature of your hand, you raise to 3NT. Pat now bids 4NT, which invites you to go on if you have anything extra. Counting points alone, you would have to classify your hand as minimum, but points are not everything. Given reasonable breaks, you could easily score eight tricks. A suit contract may play better, so you try 5♣. (Bidding naturally is a better method than showing aces.) This seems to strike a chord opposite, as Pat raises to 6♣.

West	North	East	South
Steve	*Pat*	*Edgar*	*You*
		Pass	2♣
Pass	2NT	Pass	3NT
Pass	4NT	Pass	5♣
Pass	6♣	All Pass	

West, who you will discover has a small singleton trump, leads the ♠Q. How you do plan the play?

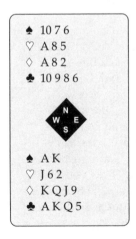

♠ 10 7 6
♡ A 8 5
◇ A 8 2
♣ 10 9 8 6

♠ A K
♡ J 6 2
◇ K Q J 9
♣ A K Q 5

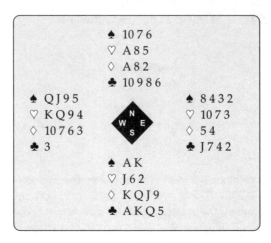

On a 3-2 trump break, the slam almost plays itself. You draw trumps in three rounds and score your last two trumps independently either by ruffing a spade in hand or, having cashed four round of diamonds, by ruffing a heart in dummy. The 4-1 split puts a spanner in the works.

With a sure heart loser, you will have to use dummy's ◊A as an entry for finessing in trumps. This just leaves you with a problem in hearts. If West has a bare king or queen or East has K-Q alone, straightforward means will do it, but none of these holdings seem likely. No endplay is possible even if East has ♡K-Q and helpful shape in the other suits. You might manage to strip Edgar's exit cards, but you lack the entry to lead a heart towards the jack to throw him in.

♠Q-J bare is a possibility, albeit a slim one, especially with Steve short in trumps. Surely, your best chance is for West to hold the ♡K-Q.

This gives you threats against him in two suits. You might like to lose a trick to 'rectify the count', but this is neither safe (they may play a heart back) nor necessary. Having drawn trumps, you run the diamonds. What can West keep? If he comes down to a doubleton heart, ace and another sets up the jack. If he bares the ♠J, you cash the king. True, you must guess which major suit he has unguarded, but you will guess right much of the time.

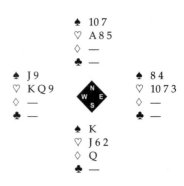

BOARD 51   Dealer: South. E/W Vulnerable.

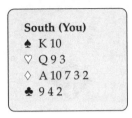

South (You)
♠ K 10
♡ Q 9 3
◇ A 10 7 3 2
♣ 9 4 2

After you and Steve both pass, Pat opens 2♡ in third position. By agreement, this shows a six-card heart suit, with a range from a good five up to a poor 10. You are aware, from general bridge knowledge rather than from any discussion, that in third seat, non-vulnerable against vulnerable, players sometimes depart from their agreed methods. Edgar overcalls 2♠ and you compete with 3♡. You do not expect to buy the contract in 3♡, but your bid makes it difficult for Steve to invite game: he cannot bid 2NT and, if he bids 3♠, it will sound like he just wants to compete. Whether from choice or expediency (you will find out in a moment), Steve jumps to 4♠ to close the auction:

West	North	East	South
Steve	*Pat*	*Edgar*	*You*
			Pass
Pass	2♡	2♠	3♡
4♠	All Pass		

You lead the ♡3 and partner's ten draws the ace.

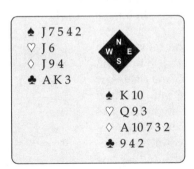

♠ J 7 5 4 2
♡ J 6
◇ J 9 4
♣ A K 3

♠ K 10
♡ Q 9 3
◇ A 10 7 3 2
♣ 9 4 2

Declarer cashes the ♠A, on which Pat drops the queen, then takes three rounds of clubs, ace-king, and low to the queen, all following. Now he leads the ♡7. How do you propose to beat the contract?

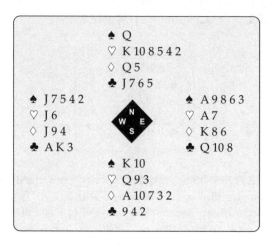

```
                    ♠ Q
                    ♡ K 10 8 5 4 2
                    ◊ Q 5
                    ♣ J 7 6 5
  ♠ J 7 5 4 2                        ♠ A 9 8 6 3
  ♡ J 6          ┌─────────┐         ♡ A 7
  ◊ J 9 4        │    N    │         ◊ K 8 6
  ♣ A K 3        │  W   E  │         ♣ Q 10 8
                 │    S    │
                 └─────────┘
                    ♠ K 10
                    ♡ Q 9 3
                    ◊ A 10 7 3 2
                    ♣ 9 4 2
```

If you have ever read one of Hugh Kelsey's highly regarded books on defensive strategy, you will know that he regarded one technique as superior to all others: counting.

In spades, you know declarer began with five, as Pat followed once and Edgar would not overcall with four. The club position, if you think about it, also seems marked. If he had the thirteenth club, declarer would have discarded dummy's losing heart on it. Most likely Pat does have a six-card heart suit, as its quality leaves a little to be desired. This means you read declarer for a 5-2-3-3 shape, or possibly 5-3-2-3. If Pat has the ◊K, you can beat the contract easily, with two diamonds, a heart and a spade. If, instead, declarer has the king and queen, no hope exists. Thus the critical position is when partner has the queen. In this case, a diamond lead from either side of the table may prove fatal, allowing your opponent to escape with one diamond loser.

You definitely do not want your side to be endplayed twice, so you win this trick with the ♡Q and cash your ♠K. If you continue with ace and another diamond, it might look like Edgar has a guess, but he knows that if you had A-Q you would have let Pat win the heart. Leading low does not help either. The answer is to lead a third heart. The predicted ruff and discard is no use and your side wins two diamonds.

```
         ♠ —
         ♡ K 8 5 4 2
         ◊ Q 5
         ♣ J
♠ J 7 5 4              ♠ 9 8 6 3
♡ J        ┌─────┐    ♡ 7
◊ J 9 4    │  N  │    ◊ K 8 6
♣ —        │W   E│    ♣ —
           │  S  │
           └─────┘
         ♠ K
         ♡ Q 9
         ◊ A 10 7 3 2
         ♣ —
```

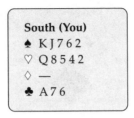

South (You)
♠ K J 7 6 2
♡ Q 8 5 4 2
♢ —
♣ A 7 6

Steve, on your left, opens 1♢ and Pat overcalls 2NT. This is the unusual no-trump, showing at least five cards in the two lowest unbid suits, hearts and clubs. Edgar jumps all the way to 5♢.

With five-card heart support and a partial fit in clubs as well, it would seem cowardly to pass. True, the spade holding looks more valuable if you defend, but the other features of the hand, especially the diamond void, suggest declaring. You bid 5♡ and there is no further bidding.

West	North	East	South
Steve	*Pat*	*Edgar*	*You*
1♢	2NT	5♢	5♡
All Pass			

Steve strokes his 5 o'clock shadow a couple of times and leads the ♢J.

♠ 3
♡ A 9 7 6 3
♢ K 5
♣ K 9 5 3 2

♠ K J 7 6 2
♡ Q 8 5 4 2
♢ —
♣ A 7 6

You ruff the diamond and lead a trump to the ace. Both opponents follow but the king does not fall. How should you continue?

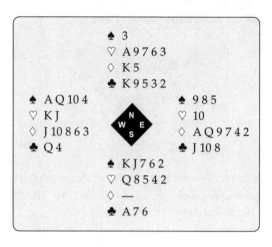

You now have the ♠A and ♡K as seemingly certain losers. To bring home the contract, you will somehow need to avoid losing a club as well. One idea is to lead dummy's singleton spade. If you find Edgar with A-Q-x, he can take the ace but a single ruff will set up the suit, allowing you to throw three clubs from dummy. A similar position would arise if Edgar has A-x-x-x. If he ducks, you can put up the king and he loses his ace; if he grabs the ace, you only need one ruff to bring down the queen as before.

Unfortunately, the bidding and early play make it virtually impossible for Edgar to hold the ♠A. The lead marks him with A-Q of diamonds, so Steve surely needs the ♠A and, very likely, the ♡K to have anything like a vulnerable opening bid. The solution is to arrange an endplay, throwing Steve in with the ♡K at a point when he has only losing leads. For this to happen, you will need him to have a doubleton club.

Ruff dummy's remaining diamond, then cash the ace and king of clubs before exiting with a trump. After taking his ♡K, what can West do? If he leads a diamond, you can take your pick: throw a club from hand or a spade from dummy or do both. A low spade exit is clearly no better for him. He can postpone the fateful moment by cashing the ♠A, but a second spade allows you to set up the suit for three club discards.

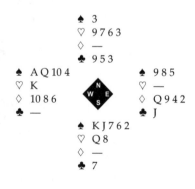

BOARD 53   Dealer: North. N/S Vulnerable.

> **South (You)**
> ♠ A K 9 5 2
> ♡ A Q 9 3
> ◇ Q
> ♣ A K 2

The first two players pass, allowing you to open 2♣, the big bid in your system. Pat, to your surprise, responds 3♣. The requirements for a positive response have changed slightly over the years; without a good suit, responder might use 2◇ as a 'waiting' bid and aim to catch up later. You could bid your spades but raising clubs will simplify matters if, as is likely, you belong in clubs. Pat cue bids 4◇ and Roman Key Card Blackwood from you uncovers the ♣Q and the ◇A. So, trusting the 3♣ response to indicate better than ♣Q-x-x-x-x, you bid 7♣.

West	North	East	South
Steve	*Pat*	*Edgar*	*You*
	Pass	Pass	2♣
Pass	3♣	Pass	4♣
Pass	4◇	Pass	4NT
Pass	5◇	Pass	5♡
Pass	5NT	Pass	7♣
All Pass			

West leads the ♣8. How you do plan the play?

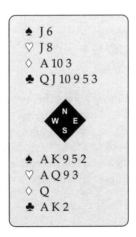

> ♠ J 6
> ♡ J 8
> ◇ A 10 3
> ♣ Q J 10 9 5 3
>
>   N
>   W   E
>   S
>
> ♠ A K 9 5 2
> ♡ A Q 9 3
> ◇ Q
> ♣ A K 2

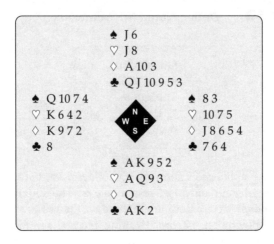

The contract appears sound and you should feel glad that you bid it even though there are only ten top tricks. If the spades break 3-3, a single ruff will set up the suit to create two winners and a diamond ruff will give you your thirteenth trick. If spades do not break quite so kindly, you will presumably need to ruff twice, and you will need either a second diamond ruff or possibly a successful heart finesse to compensate.

Nobody likes to take a finesse in a grand slam, so you concentrate on the theme of ruffing two spades and two diamonds. Let us say you win the club in hand, and play ace, king and a third spade. West follows, so you ruff high, but East discards. You now play the ace and ruff a diamond, and ruff a second spade high. Oops! This is not any good, if you ruff a second diamond, you will be stuck in hand, forced to ruff the long spade!

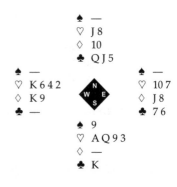

A slight variation in the timing solves this problem and spares you from relying on the heart finesse. Winning the first trick in hand is correct, but next you should take the ◊A and ruff a diamond. Only having done this do you play three rounds of spades. After ruffing the third spade high, you ruff a second diamond and a second spade, high again. With the lead now in dummy, you can draw the missing trumps, cross to the ♡A and enjoy the long spade.

South (You)
♠ 4
♡ 10 9 8 2
◊ A K Q J 8 3
♣ 10 9

Edgar on your right opens 1♠ and you hold this collection. To bring the heart suit into the equation, you would like to double, but the way you (and many people) play, doubling followed by bidding diamonds next time would show a better hand than this. If Steve raises to 2♠, Pat can make a competitive double, so you will not necessarily lose a heart fit. In practice, Steve jumps to 3♠ over your 2◊. In their traditional rubber bridge style, this shows a limit raise, inviting game, the same as it would without the overcall. All the other pairs in the match would treat this jump as pre-emptive, with a cue-bid used to indicate a decent hand containing spade support. Edgar proceeds to 4♠, ending the auction.

West	North	East	South
Steve	*Pat*	*Edgar*	*You*
		1♠	2◊
3♠	Pass	4♠	All Pass

You lead the ◊A and find that Steve has quite a solid raise. 'Thank you, partner,' Edgar says, while adjusting his cuff-links.

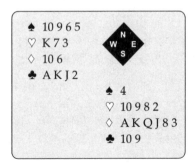

♠ 10 9 6 5
♡ K 7 3
◊ 10 6
♣ A K J 2

♠ 4
♡ 10 9 8 2
◊ A K Q J 8 3
♣ 10 9

Partner follows to the first trick with the ◊2 (a low card discourages). Unperturbed, you continue with the ◊J and Pat plays the four this time. How should you continue?

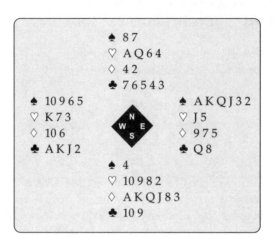

```
                    ♠ 8 7
                    ♡ A Q 6 4
                    ◊ 4 2
                    ♣ 7 6 5 4 3
   ♠ 10 9 6 5                        ♠ A K Q J 3 2
   ♡ K 7 3              N            ♡ J 5
   ◊ 10 6           W      E         ◊ 9 7 5
   ♣ A K J 2            S            ♣ Q 8
                    ♠ 4
                    ♡ 10 9 8 2
                    ◊ A K Q J 8 3
                    ♣ 10 9
```

Knowing you have a sound player opposite, this one looks easy. The first diamond discourages, presumably from a three-card holding, and the second indicates suit-preference between hearts and clubs. As the four was the lowest diamond out, it would seem that this must be the lower of Pat's remaining diamonds and so request a club switch.

Certainly, partner could have the clubs covered (within the context of dummy's holding), though one struggles to see how a club switch will prove vital. If, for example, Edgar has ♡A-Q-x, three low clubs and a third-round trump loser, a club now will not protect Pat from a throw-in.

On most layouts a heart shift appears safe, at worst saving declarer a guess of which finesse to take, if he has ♡A-J and ♣x-x-x or possibly ♡A-J-x and two low clubs (though then it would be unnatural for him to finesse in clubs). Alas, in both cases partner's signal may have given the game away already. Other than that, after fifty-three boards it may not be as easy to remember the significance of each card played; can you see an alternative explanation for partner's carding in the diamond suit?

Pat might possess a collection of trumps lower than dummy's ten, and a doubleton diamond, and have foreseen the result of encouraging you to play an unproductive third round of diamonds. If Edgar has the ♣Q and five or more running spades, he would have at least nine tricks in the black suits and a diamond ruff for a tenth. To give your side a chance of cashing the first four tricks, it was essential to play low on the ◊A to dissuade you from continuing the suit. So, as Pat's play on the second round may have been forced (as the remaining card of a doubleton), you cannot read it as necessarily suit-preference. So, shift to the ♡10.

BOARD 55   Dealer: South. Game All.

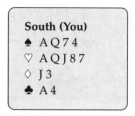

South (You)
♠ A Q 7 4
♡ A Q J 8 7
◇ J 3
♣ A 4

You open 1♡, Steve overcalls 1♠ and Pat raises to 2♡. After Edgar passes, what do you rebid?

With 18 points and five losers it would seem conservative only to invite game, even allowing for the fact that the ♠Q has lost some of its value. You have strong spades, but a hand with two doubletons does not usually play well in 3NT. If Pat holds a doubleton spade, you should be able to ruff two spades in dummy; if not, there may be a weakness in one of the minors. If you bid 3NT, Pat would pass on most hands with three-card support, often leaving you in the wrong spot. So, you bid 4♡.

West	North	East	South
Steve	*Pat*	*Edgar*	*You*
			1♡
1♠	2♡	Pass	4♡
All Pass			

West leads the ♣9. How you do plan the play?

♠ J
♡ 10 9 2
◇ Q 8 5 4 2
♣ K J 5 3

♠ A Q 7 4
♡ A Q J 8 7
◇ J 3
♣ A 4

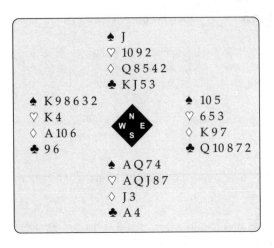

<table>
<tr><td></td><td>♠ J</td><td></td></tr>
<tr><td></td><td>♡ 10 9 2</td><td></td></tr>
<tr><td></td><td>◇ Q 8 5 4 2</td><td></td></tr>
<tr><td></td><td>♣ K J 5 3</td><td></td></tr>
</table>

♠ K 9 8 6 3 2   N   ♠ 10 5
♡ K 4   W   E   ♡ 6 5 3
◇ A 10 6   S   ◇ K 9 7
♣ 9 6   ♣ Q 10 8 7 2

♠ A Q 7 4
♡ A Q J 8 7
◇ J 3
♣ A 4

You have two diamond losers, a probable heart loser and potentially as many as three spade losers. If Steve has the ♣Q, a finesse of the ♣J will succeed and allow you to discard one of your losers. However, from his lead of the ♣9, you feel inclined to place him with a doubleton. If the ace and king of diamonds lie in one hand, or possibly if they are divided but Steve has four, you might manage to set up a trick or two in diamonds. Unfortunately, as Steve has not led a diamond, it seems unlikely that he holds both top diamonds, and, given the bidding, it appears equally improbable that Edgar holds both. Come to think of it, once you place Edgar with the ♣Q and the ◇A or ◇K, Steve sounds pretty well marked with the major-suit kings for his vulnerable overcall.

If you do feel confident Steve has the ♡K, ruffing spades in dummy sounds attractive. Unless the suit breaks 7-1, you should be able ruff three times without suffering an overruff. You must, though, take care with entries. Suppose you try the ♣J at trick one and capture the ♣Q with the ace. You can play ace and another spade, ruffing, return to hand by cashing the ♣K and ruffing a club with the ♡A, and then ruff a second spade. To get back to hand, you ruff another club, but Steve overruffs with the king and returns a trump, removing dummy's last trump. True, you could try ruffing the third club low, hoping Steve has three clubs, but this also fails with the layout as shown in the diagram.

Accepting the slight risk of a 6-1 club break, you should put up the ♣K, then play a spade to the ace, ruff a spade, return to the ♣A and ruff another spade. As the cards lie, East shows out but cannot overruff. Next, you ruff a club with the *ace*, and ruff your last spade. Steve can overruff the fourth round of clubs if he likes, but he can do you no harm, as you have already disposed of all your spades.

Dealer: West. Love All.

South (You)
♠ A K Q J 10 2
♡ 6
◇ Q J 6 4 2
♣ K

In fourth seat, you wonder what exciting things will happen before the bidding comes round. Well, Steve opens 1♡ and Edgar jumps to 4♡.

Although doubling could work well (if Pat produces secondary values in hearts and clubs), it would seem an extreme view to take. Even if you really want to create a swing (because you are losing), it still makes sense to bid 4♠. Maybe your opponents will misdefend or misjudge any subsequent bidding. In practice, your 4♠ bid ends the auction.

West	North	East	South
Steve	*Pat*	*Edgar*	*You*
1♡	Pass	4♡	4♠
All Pass			

West leads the ♡A and Pat puts down quite a suitable dummy.

♠ 8 4
♡ 10 5
◇ 9 7 5 3
♣ A J 7 6 3

♠ A K Q J 10 2
♡ 6
◇ Q J 6 4 2
♣ K

East plays the ♡2 but Steve continues with a second top heart. You ruff and cash one high trump, all following. How do you continue?

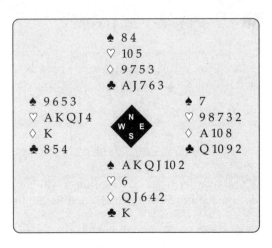

```
                    ♠ 8 4
                    ♡ 10 5
                    ◇ 9 7 5 3
                    ♣ A J 7 6 3
  ♠ 9 6 5 3                      ♠ 7
  ♡ A K Q J 4        N           ♡ 9 8 7 3 2
  ◇ K           W    E           ◇ A 10 8
  ♣ 8 5 4            S           ♣ Q 10 9 2
                    ♠ A K Q J 10 2
                    ♡ 6
                    ◇ Q J 6 4 2
                    ♣ K
```

If trumps are 3-2 and diamonds 2-2, you can simply draw trumps and knock out the ◇A-K. Needless to say, when a pair of solid bidders like Steve and Edgar bid to the four level on the minority of points at equal vulnerability, you expect uneven breaks. Edgar in particular sounds likely to hold a singleton (or a void, but you cannot cater for that) to justify jumping to 4♡ on roughly seven high-card points.

The danger in cashing a second trump is that someone will show out. Then you will lose control, as the defenders must get in twice and you will have only one trump available for ruffing. The main risk in turning to diamonds is that someone has a small singleton and can score a ruff. Which poses the greater threat?

Other things being equal, a 4-1 spade split is a 28% chance and a 3-1 diamond split with the eight or ten in the singleton is a 25% chance. The bidding and play to date confirm that the former is more likely. Steve, surely, cannot have ◇A-K-x, since (a) he would have taken further action over 4♠, (b) he might have tried a diamond at trick two, and (c) this would leave Edgar little for his raise. Also, if Edgar has ◇A-K-x, Steve might have led his diamond at trick two. Finally, Steve's actual sequence of plays, forcing you to ruff, half suggests that he can picture a 4-1 trump break.

Since playing diamonds means assuming a 2-2 break or a bare ace or king, lead a *low* one at trick four. Steve wins with the king but playing a heart does him no good: you ruff in dummy, discarding a diamond from hand, then cross to the ♣K to finish drawing trumps. Note that leading the ◇Q will not work. Unless West kindly shifts to a trump, you cannot draw trumps and later use the ♣A to play diamonds again.

RESULTS ON BOARDS 49-56

Chris and Alex, who have just played East-West in the closed room, arrive looking fairly content. 'You had the cards there!' exclaims Alex. 'We think they missed the boat on a couple of slam deals', Chris adds.

Team-mates started with a good result. On Board 49, they bid to 4♡ and, when Suzanne switched to a low diamond at trick two, made the contract by means of the squeeze we discussed. So, if you returned the ◇9 or ◇J, you can gain 10 IMPs; if not, the board is flat.

On Board 50 Lucy and Suzanne only bid as high as 4NT after Lucy decided not to respond 2NT; missing their club fit, they scored 660. So, if you found the criss-cross squeeze without the count to make 6♣, you gain 12 IMPs. If, unfortunately, you went down, you lose 13.

On Board 51, almost for the first time in the match, the bidding and play in the two rooms took the same path. Suzanne duly made the right moves at the end. So, you needed to defend correctly to flatten the board. If not, you lose 12 IMPs. You may wish to note that neither North gave a count signal in clubs. On the

North (Lucy)
♠ Q
♡ K 10 8 5 4 2
◇ Q 5
♣ J 7 6 5

actual deal it may make no difference, but with A-K-x on view in dummy, a signal would be more likely to help declarer.

On Board 52, team-mates did well, securing the contract in 5◇ doubled when Suzanne and Lucy were reluctant to go up to the five level. Lucy, North, led the ♠3, which bore all of the earmarks of a singleton. Alex played low from dummy and Suzanne made the fine play of covering the five with the six. Had she played high, Alex could have scored four spade tricks and taken the trump finesse to make 5◇.

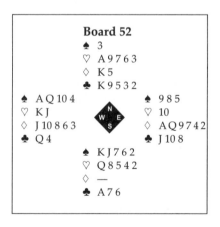

Board 52
♠ 3
♡ A 9 7 6 3
◇ K 5
♣ K 9 5 3 2

♠ A Q 10 4   ♠ 9 8 5
♡ K J   ♡ 10
◇ J 10 8 6 3   ◇ A Q 9 7 4 2
♣ Q 4   ♣ J 10 8

♠ K J 7 6 2
♡ Q 8 5 4 2
◇ —
♣ A 7 6

As things went, team-mates registered –200. This gives you the chance to gain 10 IMPs by making 5♡; if you went one down, you lose 7.

On Board 53 the auction started 2♣-3♣, as it did in yours, but then Suzanne rebid 3♠ and Lucy, with a difficult bid, raised to 4♠. After this start, they did well to avoid playing in spades, which they just managed because Suzanne bid 6♣ next. There they played, scoring 1370. So, if you made 7♣, you win 13 IMPs; if you went down, you lose 16.

On Board 54 Alex and Chris bid to 4♠ using the cue-bid to show a value raise as we discussed. Suzanne and Lucy then defended well, with the latter correctly not playing high-low in diamonds and the former finding the heart switch. This means that duplicating what happened there is the best you can do on the board. If you allowed declarer to make 4♠ (with an overtrick no doubt), you lose 13 IMPs.

On Board 55, Suzanne was also in 4♡, but she played too quickly at trick one, finessing dummy's ♣J. This meant that Alex could overruff a club and return a trump, preventing one of the three ruffs vital for the contract's success. So you gain 12 IMPs if you made 4♡ or lose 3 if you went two down (unlikely); one down gives a flat board.

On Board 56, Alex, as West, envisaging very few spades in Chris's hand, ploughed on to 5♡ rather than defending 4♠ as Steve did. With North-South not doubling and unable to take a club ruff, this went quietly one down. This means you gain 9 IMPs if you made 4♠, lose 3 if you went one down (attacking diamonds with the ◇Q) or lose 4 if you went two down (drawing two rounds of trumps).

Board 56
♠ 8 4
♡ 10 5
◇ 9 7 5 3
♣ A J 7 6 3

♠ 9 6 5 3
♡ A K Q J 4
◇ K
♣ 8 5 4

♠ 7
♡ 9 8 7 3 2
◇ A 10 8
♣ Q 10 9 2

♠ A K Q J 10 2
♡ 6
◇ Q J 6 4 2
♣ K

If you have played well, your opponents will be debating whether to play the last set. If you lead by 50-60 IMPs (or more) they might well concede (and get home at a respectable hour!). It is most unlikely that they will win this amount over eight boards, especially as such a score would imply that you are the better team. It would take some very swingy boards (you may have noticed that I have included a higher than average number of those to make the match interesting) and a lot of right views to turn the match round. Anyway, the news has come in: Lucy and Suzanne want to play you and Pat in the open room, whilst Wayne and Sally will tackle Sam and Phil in the closed. Good luck!

BOARD 57   Dealer: North. E/W Vulnerable.

South (You)
♠ A 9 7 6 4 3
♡ A K 9 2
◊ 5 4
♣ 10

You open 1♠ in third seat after two passes. Lucy overcalls 2♣, Pat raises you to 2♠ and Suzanne raises her partner to 3♣. What do you bid?

Counting points alone would lead you to value the hand as minimum and not worth a further bid. Shape is, of course, just as important, and hands containing ten cards between the two longest suits usually play well; Ron Klinger said as much with his 'six-four bid more' tip. No matter what the vulnerability you should compete to 3♠. Partner will not place you with too much, as you would bid 3♡ (or 3◊) to invite game. Lucy jumps to 5♣ over 3♠, thus ending the auction.

West	North	East	South
Lucy	Pat	Suzanne	You
	Pass	Pass	1♠
2♣	2♠	3♣	3♠
5♣	All Pass		

Pat leads the ♠Q, and dummy's assets, though modest, pose a real threat; you would have liked to see the ♠K and fewer hearts.

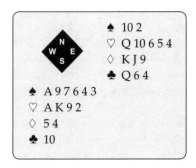

♠ 10 2
♡ Q 10 6 5 4
◊ K J 9
♣ Q 6 4

♠ A 9 7 6 4 3
♡ A K 9 2
◊ 5 4
♣ 10

How do you plan to defeat this contract?

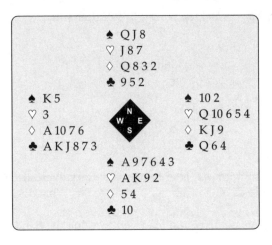

```
                    ♠ Q J 8
                    ♡ J 8 7
                    ◇ Q 8 3 2
                    ♣ 9 5 2
   ♠ K 5                          ♠ 10 2
   ♡ 3                            ♡ Q 10 6 5 4
   ◇ A 10 7 6        N            ◇ K J 9
   ♣ A K J 8 7 3   W   E          ♣ Q 6 4
                     S
                    ♠ A 9 7 6 4 3
                    ♡ A K 9 2
                    ◇ 5 4
                    ♣ 10
```

At this vulnerability, Lucy has clearly bid 5♣ hoping to make it. So she must possess the majority of the high cards you cannot see. For sure, you can beat the contract if two hearts and a spade stand up and, if the ♠K falls at trick one, this will be a realistic hope.

If you cannot rattle off three tricks in the majors, perhaps partner will produce a trump winner, the ♣K behind the ace for example. Some scope also exists to make a diamond trick if Lucy has the ace and ten of diamonds, as then she will have a two-way finesse.

Naturally, you can ill afford to lead out two top hearts if declarer has a singleton, as this will set up dummy's suit. You will want to gauge from partner's signal whether to continue hearts. Sadly, even if you judge to revert to spades, you may have given away enough for Lucy to get the diamonds right. She will read you for length in the majors and might guess that Pat would not put you up to 2♠ on ♠Q-J-x and a bust.

Indeed you already have a fairly good idea that declarer has ten cards in the minors. With a 2-2-3-6 shape, (a) she would appear short of playing strength for her 5♣ bid, and, (b) with a spade stopper and hope of running the club suit, she might well have tried 3NT.

Surely, your best bet is to win the first trick with the ♠A, cash the ♡A and, if partner follows with the lowest possible heart, casually continue with the ♡9. Since you hold the ♡2, Lucy cannot easily read Pat's first heart as discouraging and will surely place the ♡K on her left. This being the case, she might put you with the ◇Q. Who knows, she may even try a backward finesse if the ◇Q and ◇10 are missing!

BOARD 58   Dealer: East. Game All.

```
South (You)
♠ A J 8 5 3
♡ A 8 6
◊ Q 10
♣ K 10 2
```

In second seat, you open 1♠, and Pat bids 3◊, a strong jump shift. You could bid 3NT but rebidding 3♠ saves space, and you do just that. Pat continues with 4♣. In common with modern practice, you do not jump shift on a two-suited hand (except with a fit for opener's suit), so you read this as an advance cue-bid agreeing spades. You cue-bid 4♡ and next Pat bids 4NT, Roman Key Card Blackwood you may recall. You reply 5♡, showing two aces (or one and the ♠K) but denying the ♠Q. Pat then jumps to 6♠ to conclude the auction.

West	North	East	South
Lucy	*Pat*	*Suzanne*	*You*
		Pass	1♠
Pass	3◊	Pass	3♠
Pass	4♣	Pass	4♡
Pass	4NT	Pass	5♡
Pass	6♠	All Pass	

Lucy picks up her glass of mineral water and swirls it around before leading the ♡2. How you do plan the play?

```
♠ Q 6 4 2
♡ K 3
◊ A K 8 4 3
♣ A 9
```

```
        N
      W   E
        S
```

```
♠ A J 8 5 3
♡ A 8 6
◊ Q 10
♣ K 10 2
```

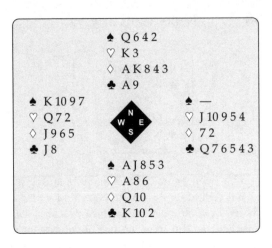

This contract appears almost lay-down, but note the 'almost'! If the lead is a singleton (or from a seven-card suit), or if someone has a minor-suit void, you can avoid any danger of a ruff by playing ace and another trump. With only four trumps missing, the partner of whoever wins the second round cannot have any trumps left. In practice, a 4-0 trump split poses a more serious danger. You can cater for four on your right by running the queen, or by leading low to the eight, or even by leading up to the queen. Can you do anything about four on your left?

You will need to strip the plain suits and arrange for Lucy to win a trump when she only has trumps left. The only way you can set this up is to start trumps with a low one to the queen, and this you do. For the strip to work she will have to be 4-3-4-2, 4-3-3-3 or 4-2-4-3. Because of the ♡2 lead and Suzanne's failure to open a weak 2♡, 4-2-4-3 seems unlikely. Sound technique allows you to cater for the other two shapes.

After the ♡A and a trump to the queen, cash the ♡K, then take two diamonds and ruff a diamond. When Lucy has four, you ruff a heart, ruff a diamond, cash the top clubs and exit with a plain card. If Lucy has only three diamonds, you ruff each minor once instead of diamonds twice. Variations are possible in the timing (or you can ruff only one diamond and duck a trump at the end); the key is to play diamonds before trying a club ruff.

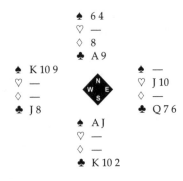

BOARD 59   Dealer: South. Love All.

> **South (You)**
> ♠ K Q 10 9 4
> ♡ K 6
> ◇ 9 3
> ♣ J 6 5 4

You pass, Lucy on your left opens 1◇, Pat passes and Suzanne responds 1♡. What action should you take?

Ordinarily, if you wish to enter the bidding when the opponents bid two suits and you hold 5-4 in the unbid suits, you do so with a take-out double. Having passed already, you certainly have the values to try to compete, but special considerations apply. Firstly, given the strength of your hand, you do not expect to buy the contract; secondly, one of your suits is much more robust than the other, giving you a clear preference for which suit you might want led. So, you decide to bid 1♠. Lucy rebids 1NT (15-17) and Suzanne raises her to game.

West	North	East	South
Lucy	*Pat*	*Suzanne*	*You*
			Pass
1◇	Pass	1♡	1♠
1NT	Pass	3NT	All Pass

Partner leads the ♠5, and dummy contains good news and bad news: the ♠J is the good; the 14 points is the bad.

Can you see any hope of defeating the contract?

> ♠ J 7 2
> ♡ A Q J 8 3
> ◇ Q J 10
> ♣ K 3
>
> ♠ K Q 10 9 4
> ♡ K 6
> ◇ 9 3
> ♣ J 6 5 4

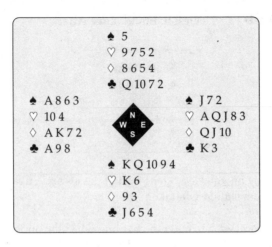

You can count declarer for all the missing aces and kings to make up her minimum of 15 points. You will have to hope that she has just four diamonds and Pat the ♣Q. This means that your opponent can count only eight top tricks – four diamonds, two clubs and two aces.

If she intends to take the heart finesse, you can win four spades and a heart. Unfortunately, your overcall may have tipped Lucy off about the location of the ♡K. If so, then rather than admitting defeat by finessing in hearts, she will aim to throw you in with a spade, hoping to score dummy's ♡A-Q on a forced heart return. Of course, she can only do this having successfully stripped your cards in the minors.

Lucy will hold up the ♠A for at least one round, so no scope exists for deceiving her about your spade length. Thankfully, though, as you did not make a take-out double, she knows nothing about your four clubs.

So, you can pretend to hold a heart more and a club less, i.e. a 5-3-2-3 shape. Having won trick one with the ♠9, continue spades to drive out the ace. Then, when declarer runs the diamonds (right), casually discard the ♡6 and the ♣4. You can continue the deception by dropping the ♣J when she cashes the ♣A-K. If she exits with a spade now, you will have a club to make at the end. If she cashes the ♡A, that is just too bad.

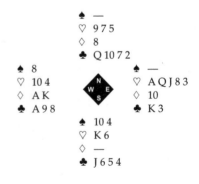

BOARD 60   Dealer: West. N/S Vulnerable.

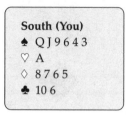

South (You)
♠ Q J 9 6 4 3
♡ A
◇ 8 7 6 5
♣ 10 6

Fourth in hand, you witness a lot of action before your turn comes to call. Lucy pre-empts with 3♡, Pat doubles (for take-out) and Suzanne bids 4◇. You happily bid 4♠ for now, knowing that for a change you have some values in reserve. You half expect an opponent to bid on, but Pat is the one to advance, with a cue-bid of 5◇ (or at any rate you take it as a cue-bid – good luck to Suzanne if she has psyched!). You admit to the ♡A with a 5♡ cue-bid and find yourself in a slam:

West	North	East	South
Lucy	*Pat*	*Suzanne*	*You*
3♡	Dbl	4◇	4♠
Pass	5◇	Pass	5♡
Pass	6♠	All Pass	

West leads the ◇2 and dummy, though strong, falls short of ideal.

♠ A K 10 7
♡ 8 5
◇ A J 10
♣ A K J 4

♠ Q J 9 6 4 3
♡ A
◇ 8 7 6 5
♣ 10 6

You have only ten tricks on top, so surely need to place West with the ♣Q, but from where can you find a twelfth? (When you play trumps, you will find that East shows out on the first round.)

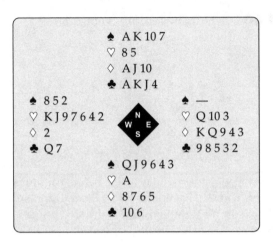

You would dearly love to duck the first trick, setting up a squeeze in the minors if East has four or more clubs. Unfortunately, West would ruff the return. Can you turn the 5-1 diamond split to your advantage?

Perhaps Lucy has ♣Q-x-x-x. Then you might strip the hand (taking the club finesse) and put her in with the fourth round, forcing her to give you a ruff and discard. This hope goes when, after you put up the ◊A and cash a round of trumps, Suzanne shows out. Prospects seem bleak now, because the club / diamond squeeze will not work. (East keeps clubs, leaving any established diamond winner marooned – top diagram).

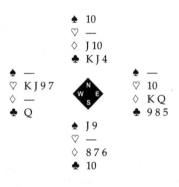

One chance is to take the ♡A, draw trumps ending in dummy and lead a heart. If East does not cover, you can discard a diamond and later squeeze her in the minors. However, it is unlikely that West has all the missing hearts down to the nine and, when East covers, you can fall back on finding Lucy with ♣Q-x. You ruff and cash the ♣A. If she keeps her ♣Q, you allow her to win a trick with it (lower diagram). If not, you have four club tricks.

Win the Big Match

Dealer: North. Game All.

> South (You)
> ♠ Q J 10 7 5 4 2
> ♡ Q
> ◇ A K 10
> ♣ K 7

Suzanne, in second seat on your right, opens 4♡. She may be pushing the boat out in an attempt to recover lost ground (if your side enjoys a healthy lead the match), but she is vulnerable and may well have a perfectly normal 4♡ opening. With this shape, to do anything other than overcall 4♠ would be perverse. Lucy doubles to end the auction:

West	North	East	South
Lucy	*Pat*	*Suzanne*	*You*
	Pass	4♡	4♠
Dbl	All Pass		

West leads the ♡2 and, at the risk of making an understatement, I can tell you that the sight of dummy comes as a disappointment.

East wins the first heart with the king and switches to the ♣10. You play low, but West wins with the ace and returns the ♣4. East ruffs this second round of clubs with the ♠3 (ouch!) and continues with the ♡J. How can you salvage something from the wreckage?

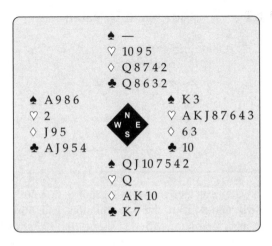

Given that Suzanne would hardly open 4♡ on a six-card suit, and Lucy would surely not lead low from a doubleton, you can read the hearts as 8-1. You have two decisions to make: (a) how high to ruff and, (b) if you win the trick, whether to lead a high trump or a low one. It seems reasonable to assume that Lucy needs four trumps or A-K-x for her double, and it will simplify our discussion if we exclude other holdings.

If West has ♠A-K-8 or ♠A-K-9, you will lose 1100 whatever you do. If you ruff high, West will overruff and later obtain a trump promotion after giving East (who will be 3-8-1-1) a diamond ruff. If you ruff low, West scores her low trump at once and East will still get her diamond ruff. Likewise, if West has ♠A-K-9-6 or ♠A-K-8-6, you must lose seven tricks. However high you ruff, West can overruff and play a club for East to uppercut.

Now we consider the chances to get out for 800. If West has ♠A-K-6, you need to ruff with the seven or higher. Then you can lead high or low. If West has ♠A-K-9-8, you do best to ruff low, though you could recover from ruffing high via double-dummy play. If West holds ♠A-9-8-6 or ♠K-9-8-6, both plays matter. You must ruff high but lead low.

This gives four likely layouts on which your play matters. On three of the four, you want to ruff high, so you will do that. Having done so, and seen West discard, you do best to lead low next (vital on two of the three layouts). Admittedly, if Lucy has doubled very aggressively with ♠A-9-8 or worse, you would do better to ruff high and lead high, but a restricted choice argument applies to further reduce the odds on a 3-3 trump break – with three trumps, East will be 3-8-1-1, and she might equally have chosen to lead her singleton diamond at trick two.

Dealer: East. Love All.

> **South (You)**
> ♠ J 9 6
> ♡ 6
> ◇ A K 7
> ♣ A J 8 5 3 2

Suzanne, the dealer, opens 2♠, systemically a six-card spade suit with a good 5 points up to a poor 10. You would prefer to have a better suit to overcall at the three level, but one cannot wait for the perfect hand, and you bid 3♣. Pat bids 3♡, forcing, and you must find another bid. 3NT could be the right contract if Pat has some help in spades, so you bid 3♠. Pat does not bid 3NT, choosing 4♣ instead. A good rule here is that if you are ever unsure, you treat a bid as forcing. So, since you intend to bid on, you might as well cue-bid 4◇. Partner seems to like the sound of this and jumps to 6♣, concluding the auction:

West	North	East	South
Lucy	*Pat*	*Suzanne*	*You*
		2♠	3♣
Pass	3♡	Pass	3♠
Pass	4♣	Pass	4◇
Pass	6♣	All Pass	

West leads the ♠8. How do you plan the play?

> ♠ A 3
> ♡ A Q J 5 4 2
> ◇ 8 6 4
> ♣ K Q
>
> ♠ J 9 6
> ♡ 6
> ◇ A K 7
> ♣ A J 8 5 3 2

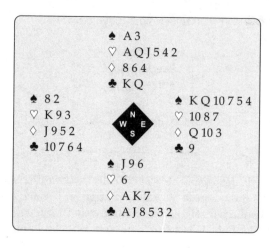

```
                ♠ A 3
                ♡ A Q J 5 4 2
                ◊ 8 6 4
                ♣ K Q
  ♠ 8 2                        ♠ K Q 10 7 5 4
  ♡ K 9 3          N           ♡ 10 8 7
  ◊ J 9 5 2     W     E        ◊ Q 10 3
  ♣ 10 7 6 4       S           ♣ 9
                ♠ J 9 6
                ♡ 6
                ◊ A K 7
                ♣ A J 8 5 3 2
```

Annoying if predictable, the opening spade lead attacks the side entry to dummy's hearts. Unless you duck the trick and Suzanne generously switches, you will probably have to forget about setting up the hearts.

You can, if you wish, ruff the third round of spades in dummy, but that still leaves you with a diamond loser. You do have a choice of taking a straight heart finesse or a ruffing finesse, and the former seems more attractive on two counts. Firstly, if Suzanne holds six spades to her partner's two, more room exists for the ♡K in Lucy's hand. Secondly, a successful ruffing finesse may do you no good if hearts split 4-2.

The big danger of ruffing a spade in dummy is that a 4-1 split will give you a trump loser. As you intend to play West for the ♡K anyway, you should forget about the spade ruff. Hearts will be a threat against West and spades one against East, leaving neither able to protect diamonds.

Duck the first spade, win the second (East must return one or you set up the hearts), unblock the ♣K-Q, cross to the ◊A and run the clubs. West must reduce to a singleton diamond to keep three hearts, and dummy throws a diamond. Then play a heart to the queen and cash the ♡A in order to squeeze East in spades and diamonds. No ambiguity arises, as if no major-suit king appears, the third diamond (the seven!) must be good.

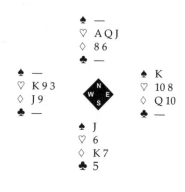

```
          ♠ —
          ♡ A Q J
          ◊ 8 6
          ♣ —
  ♠ —                  ♠ K
  ♡ K 9 3     N        ♡ 10 8
  ◊ J 9    W     E     ◊ Q 10
  ♣ —         S        ♣ —
          ♠ J
          ♡ 6
          ◊ K 7
          ♣ 5
```

BOARD 63   Dealer: South. N/S Vulnerable.

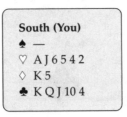

South (You)
♠ —
♡ A J 6 5 4 2
◇ K 5
♣ K Q J 10 4

You open 1♡, Lucy overcalls 1NT, Pat raises to 2♡ and Suzanne competes with 2♠. The 1NT overcall acts as a warning bell, since it increases the chance of a bad trump break and/or a losing finesse. Nevertheless, your four-loser hand gives you a safety margin. For you to bid less than 4♡ would be cowardly. (I suppose you could bid 3♣, in theory a game try, intending to bid 4♡ next whatever partner does.)

West	North	East	South
Lucy	*Pat*	*Suzanne*	*You*
			1♡
1NT	2♡	2♠	4♡
All Pass			

West leads the ♠2 and, when dummy appears, you see why nobody felt like bidding 4♠.

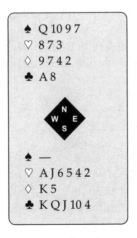

♠ Q 10 9 7
♡ 8 7 3
◇ 9 7 4 2
♣ A 8

♠ —
♡ A J 6 5 4 2
◇ K 5
♣ K Q J 10 4

You play dummy's nine and ruff East's jack – a move that seems to catch Suzanne by surprise as she inspects the trick carefully. How do you continue?

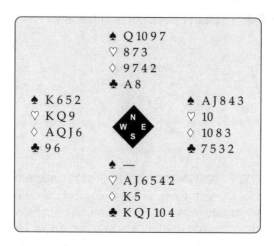

Assuming Lucy has not underled the ace-king of spades, the bidding and play to trick one enables you to place all the missing cards. Just to have a minimum of 15 points, Lucy must have ♡K-Q, a high spade (the king, presumably) and ◊A-Q (A-Q-J unless she has the ♣A). This makes it futile either to lead towards the ◊K or to finesse in trumps.

If trumps break 2-2 (i.e. West has K-Q alone), you can make eleven tricks: draw trumps, run the clubs and eventually ruff a diamond in dummy. As expected, however, when you lay down the ♡A you see the nine and ten appear. Now it looks like you have four losers: two trumps and two diamonds. Certainly, you will if you play a second round of trumps, and it must be right to abandon them at this point.

You could try running the clubs in the hope that West ruffs, in which case you could ruff a diamond after all. Can you improve on this?

Assuming you read the spades as 4-5, the first key play is to use dummy's ♣A entry to ruff a second spade. On the run of the clubs, West can spare two diamonds, whilst dummy must keep at least one spade. The fifth club is the killer; if West bares the ◊A, you duck a diamond; ruffing is no good either; she does best to come down to one spade, but you ruff in dummy (!) and ruff a spade,

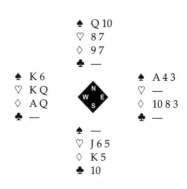

removing her exit card. A trump exit then forces her to lead a diamond.

Win the Big Match

BOARD 64   Dealer: West. E/W Vulnerable.

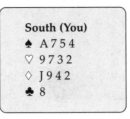

South (You)
♠ A 7 5 4
♡ 9 7 3 2
◊ J 9 4 2
♣ 8

After Lucy opens 1♡, Pat overcalls 2♡. This is a Michaels cue-bid, which you may recall shows at least five spades and at least five cards in an unspecified minor. Suzanne bids 3◊, so presumably partner's minor is clubs. Maybe you should jump to 4♠ here, applying maximum pressure on your left-hand opponent, but you decide to allow partner a little leeway with 3♠. You can only count on a nine-card fit, and the misfit in clubs warns you not to get overly excited.

Next Lucy rebids 4♡, Pat bids 4♠ and Suzanne calls 4NT, Roman Key Card Blackwood. Against a less experienced pair, you might bid 5♠ to test whether they have discussed what to do over intervention. Here, given that you have hopes of beating 6♡, you neither wish to keep them out of it nor encourage Pat to save against it. Lucy bids 5♠ (two key cards and the ♡Q) and Suzanne's 6♡ ends the auction:

West	North	East	South
Lucy	*Pat*	*Suzanne*	*You*
1♡	2♡	3◊	3♠
4♡	4♠	4NT	Pass
5♠	Pass	6♡	All Pass

Partner leads the ♠Q and declarer calls for a low card from dummy. How do you propose to defeat this slam to end the match on a high?

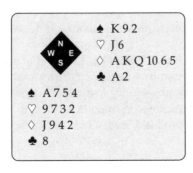

♠ K 9 2
♡ J 6
◊ A K Q 10 6 5
♣ A 2

♠ A 7 5 4
♡ 9 7 3 2
◊ J 9 4 2
♣ 8

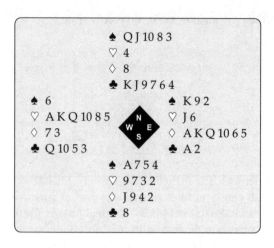

Lucy's 5♣ response marks her with the ace-king-queen of hearts, so you are not going to score a trump trick. You also know that two rounds of spades will not stand up. This leaves you with two possible ways to defeat the contract: score the ♠A in your hand and a diamond ruff in partner's, or score the ♠A and a slow club trick.

You can dismiss the idea of a diamond ruff. With a void in diamonds, Pat would surely lead an 'unusual' spade, perhaps fifth highest or the jack. The normal queen lead suggests you think of something else.

Suppose the ♠Q wins the first trick and Pat continues with the jack, declarer ruffing. She will then draw trumps and play on diamonds, ruffing one to set up the suit. Assuming Lucy has a six-card suit for her 4♡ bid, this will give her six trumps, five diamonds and the ♣A – twelve tricks. It will not even matter if she is void in diamonds (unlikely as that is). In that case, she can use the ♡J as an entry for taking the ruff needed to set up the diamonds.

Of course, with the ♣K-Q, Pat can break up the above sequence by switching to a club at trick two, defeating the contract even if Lucy has seven hearts. Can you do anything about it if declarer has the ♣Q?

Well, if Pat's clubs include the K-J (and a round of spades stand up), you can beat the slam by overtaking the first trick and switching to a club. This will remove dummy's entry and restrict declarer to eleven tricks – one spade, six trumps, three diamonds and a club. The only risk is that she has seven hearts and jack-high clubs, but the actual layout seems far more likely.

RESULTS ON BOARDS 57-64

'I am glad the match is over', says Sam smiling, coming with Phil to join you, 'not that we haven't had some good boards.' 'Indeed', says Phil.

On Board 57, the contract was the same, and Sally defended with no subtlety at all, laying down the ♡K (!) at trick two. So Sam guessed the ◊Q right. If you geared yourself up for smoothly playing a low heart at trick three, you gain 12 IMPs; if not, assume 5♣ made and a flat board.

South (You / Sally)
♠ A 9 7 6 4 3
♡ A K 9 2
◊ 5 4
♣ 10

Board 58 saw another good result for your team-mates. The contract (6♠) and the lead (the ♡2) were the same, but Sally did not spot any way to deal with four trumps offside. This means that if you found the trump endplay, you score a hard-won 17 IMPs; if not, the board is flat.

On Board 59 Phil and Sam again did well. With her 5-2-2-4 shape, Sally made the second-round take-out double that you rejected. This meant Wayne led the ♣2 against 3NT, allowing declarer eleven tricks. So, if you blanked the ♡K smoothly, you gain 11 IMPs, whilst if you let yourself be endplayed, you still gain 2. If, however, you bared the ♡K but hesitated in doing so, assume Lucy dropped it to flatten the board.

The slam you reached on Board 60 was a poor one, certainly from your side of the table, and they stopped in 5♠ in the other room, making eleven tricks. This means you gain 13 IMPs if you played West for ♣J-x and made 6♠; if not, you lose 13.

On Board 61, after Phil opened only 1♡, Sally could bid her hand without having to go to 4♠, and defended 4♡. 4♡ should go down: the defenders can take two spade ruffs and two top diamonds. In fact, Sally began with the ◊A-K, so they lost one ruff. Maybe Wayne should have dropped the ◊Q at trick one. Anyway, the 620 score means you lose 5 IMPs if you got out for 800, or 10 if you went for 1100.

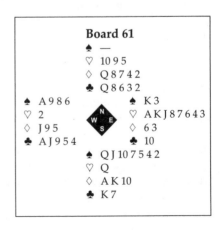

Board 61
♠ —
♡ 10 9 5
◊ Q 8 7 4 2
♣ Q 8 6 3 2

♠ A 9 8 6   ♠ K 3
♡ 2   ♡ A K J 8 7 6 4 3
◊ J 9 5   ◊ 6 3
♣ A J 9 5 4   ♣ 10

♠ Q J 10 7 5 4 2
♡ Q
◊ A K 10
♣ K 7

On Board 62, Wayne and Sally somewhat conservatively stayed out of the slam, alighting in the safe contract of 3NT by North. The ♠K lead enabled declarer to score twelve tricks and 490. This means that if you played for the double squeeze to make 6♣, you gain 10 IMPs; you lose 11 if you went either one or two down.

Given the vulnerability, you can guess the contract in the other room on Board 63: 4♠ doubled. Your team-mates got there when North did not bid over the 1NT overcall, so West could support spades at the three level over South's 3♣. Repeated club leads gave the defenders two trump tricks and 300. This result means you gain 8 IMPs if you found the tricky elimination play to make 4♡; you lose 9 if not.

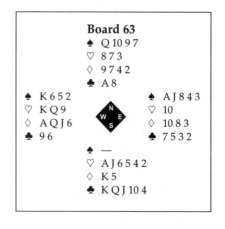

Board 63
♠ Q 10 9 7
♡ 8 7 3
◊ 9 7 4 2
♣ A 8

♠ K 6 5 2   ♠ A J 8 4 3
♡ K Q 9   ♡ 10
◊ A Q J 6   ◊ 10 8 3
♣ 9 6   ♣ 7 5 3 2

♠ —
♡ A J 6 5 4 2
◊ K 5
♣ K Q J 10 4

On Board 64, again a different side managed to secure the contract. Sam and Phil had the chance to defend 5♠ doubled and, knowing that there were bad breaks around, took it rather than pushing on to a tight slam. They won five tricks, two clubs, a trump and two aces, to pick up 500. This means that you gain 12 IMPs if you beat 6♡; if you let it make, you lose 14.

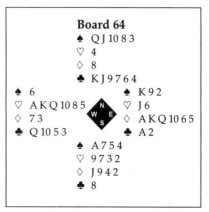

Board 64
♠ Q J 10 8 3
♡ 4
◊ 8
♣ K J 9 7 6 4

♠ 6   ♠ K 9 2
♡ A K Q 10 8 5   ♡ J 6
◊ 7 3   ◊ A K Q 10 6 5
♣ Q 10 5 3   ♣ A 2

♠ A 7 5 4
♡ 9 7 3 2
◊ J 9 4 2
♣ 8

You have now finished the match and, hopefully, the time has come to open a bottle of something suitable in celebration. (If you lost the match but won the last trick on Board 62 with the ◊7, you can celebrate that instead!) If you made the maximum number of tricks on every board, you have won the match by over 500 IMPs (and I want to know when your book is coming out!). If you lost the match (which, if you got everything wrong, you could have done by in excess of 400 IMPs) then do not worry. Although generally I steered you into a sensible contract, which can win you half the battle, a good number of the play problems were taxing, and would trouble plenty of experienced players.

SCORE-CARDS BOARDS 1 – 8

CLOSED ROOM			West Alex	North Wayne	East Chris	South Sally		
Board	Contract	By	Lead	Tricks	E/W +	E/W −	IMPs +	IMPs −
1	3NT	South	♡6	7	100			
2	2◇	South	♡10	8		90		
3	4♡	South	◇2	10		420		
4	3♡	West	♣Q	10	170			
5	4♠ x	East	◇4	7		500		
6	1NT	West	♠9	9	150			
7	3♠	South	♡K	7	200			
8	5♣	South	♡K	11		400		

OPEN ROOM			West Steve	North Pat	East Edgar	South You		
Board	Contract	By	Lead	Tricks	E/W +	E/W −	IMPs +	IMPs −
1	5♣	South	♠7					
2	4♠	South	♡10					
3	4♠ x	East	♣2					
4	4♠	South	♡Q					
5	4♡	South	♠A					
6	3NT	West	♠9					
7	4♡	East	◇A					
8	6♣	South	♡K					

DUPLICATE SCORING	
Trick scores and undertrick penalties	As in rubber bridge
Bonus for making a part score	50
Bonus for bidding and making game	300 non-vulnerable 500 vulnerable
Additional (*) bonus for bidding and making a small slam	500 non-vulnerable 750 vulnerable
Additional (*) bonus for bidding and making a grand slam	750 non-vulnerable 1500 vulnerable

* i.e. in addition to the game bonus

SCORE-CARDS BOARDS 9 – 16

CLOSED ROOM			West *Sam*	North *Edgar*	East *Phil*	South *Steve*		
Board	Contract	By	Lead	Tricks	E/W +	E/W –	IMPs +	IMPs –
9	4◇	East	♡6	11	150			
10	4♠	South	◇2	10		620		
11	3NT	East	♠8	9	400			
12	3NT	South	♡A	9		600		
13	4♠	South	♣10	9	100			
14	3♡	South	♠A	10		170		
15	2♠	South	♠5	9		140		
16	5♡ x	North	♣K	9	300			

OPEN ROOM			West *Lucy*	North *Pat*	East *Suzanne*	South *You*		
Board	Contract	By	Lead	Tricks	E/W +	E/W –	IMPs +	IMPs –
9	5◇	East	♡6					
10	4♠	South	◇2					
11	3NT x	East	♠8					
12	3NT	South	♠6					
13	4♠	South	◇7					
14	4♡	South	♠A					
15	4♠	South	♠5					
16	5♣	West	◇Q					

COMMON DUPLICATE SCORES	Non-Vulnerable	Vulnerable
3NT making 9 tricks or 5♣/5◇ making 11	400	600
4♡/4♠ making 10 tricks	420	620
1♡/1♠/2♡/2♠ making 8 tricks	110	110
1♣/1◇/2♣/2◇/3♣/3◇ making 9 tricks	110	110
1NT making 7 tricks or 2♣/2◇ making 8	90	90
1♡/1♠/2♡/2♠/3♡/3♠ making 9 tricks	140	140
4♡/4♠/5♡/5♣ making 11 tricks	450	650
3NT making 10/11 tricks respectively	430/460	630/660

SCORE-CARDS BOARDS 17 – 24

CLOSED ROOM			West *Alex*	North *Lucy*	East *Chris*	South *Suzanne*		
Board	Contract	By	Lead	Tricks	E/W +	E/W –	IMPs +	IMPs –
17	4♠	South	♡A	9	50			
18	2◇ x	West	♣10	5		500		
19	4♠	West	♣3	9		100		
20	3NT	South	◇8	12		690		
21	3NT	South	♣5	7	200			
22	5♣ x	North	♠A	9	300			
23	3NT	South	♠10	11		660		
24	6♣	East	♡5	12	920			

OPEN ROOM			West *Wayne*	North *Pat*	East *Sally*	South *You*		
Board	Contract	By	Lead	Tricks	E/W +	E/W –	IMPs +	IMPs –
17	4♠	South	♡K					
18	3NT	South	♠7					
19	4♠	West	◇10					
20	6NT	South	♠9					
21	3NT	South	♣5					
22	4♠	East	♣Q					
23	4♠ x	East	♣A					
24	6♣	West	♠5					

DUPLICATE SLAM SCORES	Non-Vulnerable	Vulnerable
6♣/6◇ making 12/13 tricks respectively	920/940	1370/1390
6♡/6♠ making 12/13 tricks respectively	980/1010	1430/1460
6NT making 12/13 tricks respectively	990/1020	1440/1470
7♣/7◇ making	1440	2140
7♡/7♠ making	1510	2210
7NT making	1520	2220

SCORE-CARDS BOARDS 25 – 32

CLOSED ROOM			West *Sam*	North *Wayne*	East *Phil*	South *Sally*		
Board	Contract	By	Lead	Tricks	E/W +	E/W –	IMPs +	IMPs –
25	3♣	South	♡7	8	50			
26	3NT	South	♠5	8	100			
27	5♡ x	South	♠10	9	300			
28	4♠ x	West	♡3	9		100		
29	3NT	South	♡2	8	100			
30	4♢	South	♣6	11		150		
31	6♠	North	♣4	11	100			
32	2♠ x	West	♣10	7		200		

OPEN ROOM			West *Lucy*	North *Pat*	East *Suzanne*	South *You*		
Board	Contract	By	Lead	Tricks	E/W +	E/W –	IMPs +	IMPs –
25	3♡	East	♢9					
26	3NT	South	♠5					
27	4♠	West	♣J					
28	4♡	South	♡10					
29	3NT	South	♡2					
30	5♢	South	♢6					
31	6♢	South	♣J					
32	2♠ x	West	♣10					

SOME DOUBLED SCORES AT DUPLICATE		
	Non-Vulnerable	Vulnerable
2♡/2♠ x making or 3♣/3♢ x making	470	670
1NT/2♣/2♢ x making	180	180
3♡/3♠ x making 9/10 tricks respectively	530/630	730/930
4♡/4♠ x making 10/11 tricks respectively	590/690	790/990
3NT/5♣/5♢ x making	550	750
5♡/5♠ x making 11/12 tricks respectively	650/750	850/1050
6♣/6♢ x making 12/13 tricks respectively	1090/1190	1540/1740
6♡/6♠ x making 12/13 tricks respectively	1210/1310	1660/1860

Win the Big Match

SCORE-CARDS BOARDS 33 – 40

CLOSED ROOM			West *Alex*	North *Lucy*	East *Chris*	South *Suzanne*		
Board	Contract	By	Lead	Tricks	E/W +	E/W –	IMPs +	IMPs –
33	5♡ x	West	◊5	9		300		
34	3NT	South	◊7	8	100			
35	4♠	East	♡A	10	620			
36	4♠	South	◊Q	9	100			
37	4♠	South	♡J	11		650		
38	2♠	West	♣K	9	140			
39	5♠	North	◊J	8	300			
40	3♡	West	♣7	8		50		

OPEN ROOM			West *Steve*	North *Pat*	East *Edgar*	South *You*		
Board	Contract	By	Lead	Tricks	E/W +	E/W –	IMPs +	IMPs –
33	4♠	South	♡K					
34	3NT	South	◊7					
35	4♠	East	♡A					
36	4♠	South	♡2					
37	6♠	South	♡J					
38	3♠	West	♣K					
39	5◊	East	♠A					
40	3♣	South	♠A					

INTERNATIONAL MATCH-POINTS (IMP) SCALE					
0 - 10	0 IMPs	370 - 420	9 IMPs	1750 - 1990	18 IMPs
20 - 40	1 IMPs	430 - 490	10 IMPs	2000 - 2240	19 IMPs
50 - 80	2 IMPs	500 - 590	11 IMPs	2250 - 2490	20 IMPs
90 - 120	3 IMPs	600 - 740	12 IMPs	2500 - 2990	21 IMPs
130 - 160	4 IMPs	750 - 990	13 IMPs	3000 - 3490	22 IMPs
170 - 210	5 IMPs	1000 - 1090	14 IMPs	3500 - 3990	23 IMPs
220 - 260	6 IMPs	1100 - 1290	15 IMPs	4000 +	24 IMPs
270 - 310	7 IMPs	1300 - 1490	16 IMPs		
320 - 360	8 IMPs	1500 - 1740	17 IMPs		

SCORE-CARDS BOARDS 41 – 48

CLOSED ROOM		West *Sam*	North *Edgar*	East *Phil*	South *Steve*			
Board	Contract	By	Lead	Tricks	E/W +	E/W –	IMPs +	IMPs –
41	4♠	West	◊5	8		200		
42	4♡ x	East	♠J	10	790			
43	5♠ x	West	◊A	9		300		
44	3NT	South	♠K	7	200			
45	7NT	South	♡J	13		2220		
46	4♠	South	◊7	10		420		
47	6♡	South	♠3	12		1430		
48	3NT	West	♣2	9	600			

OPEN ROOM		West *Wayne*	North *Pat*	East *Sally*	South *You*			
Board	Contract	By	Lead	Tricks	E/W +	E/W –	IMPs +	IMPs –
41	4♠	West	♡K					
42	4♡ x	East	♣J					
43	5◊	South	♠K					
44	3NT	South	♠K					
45	7♣	South	♡J					
46	4♠	South	♡10					
47	6♡	South	♡9					
48	3NT x	West	♠7					

SOME SAMPLE IMP SCORES			
Room 1	Room 2	Non-Vulnerable	Vulnerable
N/S make 4♡	N/S make 3♡+1	420-170 = 5 IMPs	620-170 = 10 IMPs
N/S make 4♡	N/S in 4♡-1	420+50 = 10 IMPs	620+100 = 12 IMPs
N/S make 3♣	E/W make 3◊	110+110 = 6 IMPs	same as non-vul.
N/S make 1NT	N/S in 1NT-1	90+50 = 4 IMPs	90+100 = 5 IMPs
N/S make 6◊	N/S make 5◊+1	920-420 = 10 IMPs	1370-620 = 13 IMPs
N/S make 4♠ x	N/S make 4♠	590-420 = 5 IMPs	790-620 = 5 IMPs
N/S make 2♠ x	N/S make 2♠	470-110 = 8 IMPs	670-110 = 11 IMPs
N/S make 7♣	N/S make 6♣+1	1440-940 = 11 IMPs	2140-1390=13 IMPs

SCORE-CARDS BOARDS 49 – 56

CLOSED ROOM			West Alex	North Lucy	East Chris	South Suzanne		
Board	Contract	By	Lead	Tricks	E/W +	E/W −	IMPs +	IMPs −
49	4♡	West	♠5	10	420			
50	4NT	South	♠Q	11		660		
51	4♠	East	♡3	9		100		
52	5♢ x	West	♠3	10		200		
53	6♣	South	♢2	12		1370		
54	4♠	East	♢A	9		100		
55	4♡	South	♣9	9	100			
56	5♡	West	♠8	10		50		

OPEN ROOM			West Steve	North Pat	East Edgar	South You		
Board	Contract	By	Lead	Tricks	E/W +	E/W −	IMPs +	IMPs −
49	4♡	West	♠5					
50	6♣	South	♠Q					
51	4♠	East	♡3					
52	5♡	South	♢J					
53	7♣	South	♣8					
54	4♠	East	♢A					
55	4♡	South	♣9					
56	4♠	South	♡A					

ODDS REQUIRED FOR TRYING FOR A HIGHER SCORE AT IMPS	Non-Vulnerable	Vulnerable
Bidding game instead of safe part-score	50% *	40% *
Bidding small slam instead of safe game	54% *	54% *
Bidding grand slam instead of safe small slam	60% *	61% *
Grand slam instead of game on a '5 or 7' deal	49% *	48% *
Doubling game for 1 down instead of passing	74% **	65% **
Doubling into game for 1 down instead of passing	85% **	84% **

* Includes a 5% margin in case you go more than one down or are doubled or they are in a silly contract in the other room or ** they redouble or make an overtrick.

SCORE-CARDS BOARDS 57 – 64

CLOSED ROOM		West _Sam_	North _Wayne_	East _Phil_	South _Sally_			
Board	Contract	By	Lead	Tricks	E/W +	E/W −	IMPs +	IMPs −
57	5♣	West	♠Q	11	600			
58	6♠	South	♡2	11	100			
59	3NT	West	♣2	11	460			
60	5♠	South	◇2	11		650		
61	4♡	East	◇K	10	620			
62	3NT	North	♠K	12		490		
63	4♠ x	East	♣K	8		300		
64	5♠ x	South	♡A	8	500			

OPEN ROOM		West _Lucy_	North _Pat_	East _Suzanne_	South _You_			
Board	Contract	By	Lead	Tricks	E/W +	E/W −	IMPs +	IMPs −
57	5♣	West	♠Q					
58	6♠	South	♡2					
59	3NT	West	♠5					
60	6♠	South	◇2					
61	4♠ x	South	♡2					
62	6♣	South	♠8					
63	4♡	South	♠2					
64	6♡	West	♠Q					

FINAL SCORE	1-8	9-16	17-24	25-32	33-40	41-48	59-56	57-64
+256 or more	Are you sure that you have not read this book before?							
+64 to +255	Do any professional teams or selectors know of your talents?							
+1 to +63	Congratulations. You have won a tough match.							
0	Sorry! There was no space for including tie-break boards.							
–32 to –1	A narrow loss helps to build character.							
–96 to –33	Well tried. The problems were tricky. Better luck next time.							
–160 to –97	I admire your honesty but your technique could be improved.							
–161 or worse	Have you ever thought of taking up chess or backgammon?							